JAKO
BOOKS

Also by Anderson Reynolds

The Stall Keeper (novel, 2017)

The Struggle For Survival: an historical, political and socioeconomic perspective of St. Lucia (2003)

Death by Fire (novel, 2001)

For my mother, Philomene Reynolds, in appreciation of her unflinching love and indomitable spirit.

My Father
Is No Longer There

ANDERSON REYNOLDS

JAKO BOOKS

New York, London, Toronto, Vieux Fort

Published in the United States by Jako Books, a division of
Jako Productions.

First Jako Books Edition, August 2019
www.jakoproductions.com

LCCN: 2019900269

ISBN: 978-0-9704432-7-4

Printed in Canada

Special thanks to Modeste Downes, Allan Weekes, Cedric George, Brian Francis, Dr. Jolien Harmsen, Peter Lansiquot, Dr. Prosper Raynold, and Afferton Raynold for their helpful comments and suggestions. My Father Is No Longer There has benefited much from their input.

My Father
Is No Longer There

My Father Is No Longer There

ON THE WET MORNING of June 6, 2002, a car driven by a twenty-four-year-old motorist spun out of control, ricocheted off another vehicle and plunged into my seventy-eight-year-old dad, who was on his regular morning walk alongside St. Jude's Highway, on the outskirts of Vieux Fort, a town at the southernmost tip of St. Lucia. My dad was only a few hundred yards from his home. He died on the spot. The autopsy revealed a broken neck, a broken spinal cord, and a punctured heart. The autopsy also revealed my dad had no recognizable ills: no cancer, no brain tumor, no hardening of the arteries. So it seems if not for the accident my dad would have enjoyed a good many more years.

Ironically, a few months before the accident my dad had admonished me against jogging alongside the highway. Ironically, my dad who had been a Seventh Day Adventist for more than fifty years was temperate in all things. He didn't smoke, he didn't consume alcohol, he exercised regularly, he rested on the seventh day and kept it holy, he went to bed before 9PM and was up by 6AM, and for the previous fifteen, twenty years, ate no meat. Ironically, my dad who had been an active motorist most of his adult life during which he was involved in but one accident, was killed by a motorist in the period of his life when he had long given up driving, when his early morning walk was one of the few times he ventured out of his home. Ironically, my dad who cared so much about life that a cockroach would pass near him and he would make no attempt to squash it, and who when we were children would get angry at us for killing earthworms, butterflies, birds, toads, suffered the most violent of deaths.

How can I explain my father's death? How can I explain this sorrow, this pain, this emptiness? How can I explain that one morning my father was well and walking, and the next morning no amount of coaxing, no amount of medicine, no amount of obeah, no amount of voodoo could cause him to get up?

The Saturday following the accident that took my father's life I went to the morgue at Victoria Hospital in the capital city of Castries to identify my father. I only had to take one glance to realize that the man lying there naked, save for a cloth to cover his private parts, wasn't my dad. Since the police said I had to identify the body, I lied to them and said the man was my father, then I hurried out. I wasn't about to witness the autopsy, the disembodiment of the stranger lying there as if willing the doctor to commit more violence on him than had the twenty-four-year-old. I was afraid of the long-term damage that would cause me. I was afraid of staying half-awake all night, having nightmares, thinking, dreaming of my father's body parts. I couldn't take the chance. I didn't want to remember my father in terms of body parts.

But true to form, my older brother, the fourth of my father's nine children, who had accompanied me to the morgue, and who from childhood had exhibited a boldness unbeknown to most of his brothers and sisters, seized the rare opportunity of a close-up view of an autopsy. I don't know if watching the disembodiment of his father had any negative, short or long-term, effect on him. I never asked and there hasn't been much discussion in my family about my father's death. Collectively, we planned and executed the funeral service, the burial, the wake, but it seems it was left to each of us to deal with the loss in our own individual ways. I don't know if that is always the case. But I suspect nothing can be more personal, both for the dead and the mourners, than death.

Later I furnished the police with a signed report of identification. The report, which follows, was also a lie.

Please be informed that I, Dr. Anderson Reynolds, residing in Vieux Fort, son of the late St. Brice Reynolds, was present Saturday, June 8, at the morgue at Victoria Hospital, at 9:25 a.m., where, upon the request of Officer Donat (PC 499 Donat), I identified a body as that belonging to the late St. Brice Reynolds.

I WENT TO THE FUNERAL HOME for the viewing of the man everyone said was my father. There was a man in the coffin dressed in black suit, white shirt, and red tie. Dressed as if for a wedding, but by the contentment on his face it was clear he wasn't going to any wedding. One glance told me the man lying there dressed for a wedding that would never take place wasn't my father. So I didn't stare at him; I didn't memorize every contour of his face for times of starvation. Instead I walked around the room and stared at portraits that had nothing to say to me.

In the days leading to the funeral and the weeks following the funeral, I could barely speak to anyone; I was always on the verge of tears. I couldn't properly acknowledge people's expressions of sympathy, for it took everything in me to stop the tears.

For the funeral service, my five brothers and I carried the coffin to the entrance of the church, then we wheeled it to the front. After the service we retraced our steps with the coffin. But all the while I was being a hypocrite, pretending that the man who had allowed someone else to dress him as if for a wedding, but too well for a wedding, and then enclosed him in a coffin as if he were a vampire, was my father.

At the burial, I watched as the casket descended to the bottom of the four-chamber tomb (this was the first death in my family). I watched but knew this wasn't my father descending into this hellhole, because I knew ten feet under the ground was no place for my father. I knew if my father was going anywhere it would have to be up in the heavens. My mother wasn't fooled either. She knew this man someone had played a prank on, dressing him the same way my father had dressed when he married her, wasn't her husband at all. So she would have nothing to do with the burial, she refused to see the impostor descending into the tomb. Instead, she sat in a car parked a good distance away.

At the funeral service, my brother, the eighth child of my father's nine children, the one who is a university professor of economics, gave this eulogy for my father:

Brothers and Sisters, Ladies and Gentlemen. Our father was a humble man whose lifelong journey along the narrow path to God's kingdom is now complete. He has arrived. He is at peace.

Our father traveled along this path with great discipline, quiet dignity, immense courage, and unwavering compassion for both friend and foe. I believe the evidence before us demonstrates and history will record that he was a true and faithful servant of God, of his family, and of the many people whose lives he touched. Our father organized his life around two pillars: his family and his church. In addition, he relied on his unconditional belief in the grace of God to keep these pillars upright and connected. Therefore, developing an appropriate perspective on the life we have gathered to honor today, requires an understanding of the nature of his contributions with respect to each of these pillars.

Our father embraced his responsibilities to his family without reservation. His love and devotion to us was not typically expressed via grand gestures or flamboyant demonstrations of affection. Instead, the depth of his love and commitment to us was left to be inferred from his daily devotion and determination to make any sacrifice and bear numerous burdens in the performance of his duty as both husband and father. As with everything in his life, his conception of his responsibilities as a husband and father was fundamentally informed by the understanding of God's will that he derived from his lifelong and daily study of the Word.

In a world in which we are increasingly inundated with images of grandeur and flamboyance, and in which occasional and flamboyant demonstrations of affection threaten to substitute for the things that make families work, such as acceptance of responsibility and devotion to duty, our father opted in favor of daily de-

7

votion to duty. Day by day he met every challenge with steely but compassionate resolve, responded to opportunities with understated optimism and approached all issues, big and small, with the utmost integrity. And so, with the desire to be like Jesus as his guide, with our mother as his partner, and with the Almighty's benevolence, this family and its legacy was built day by day, son by son, daughter by daughter, and lesson by lesson. It is very fitting that we should gather in this particular temple whose construction so elegantly captures the essence of what our father stood for. Brother Si's hand was steady and patient; he was consistent; and he could be relied upon to stay the course even under the most tasking circumstances. Ironically, the abruptness of his departure requires us to exhibit similar attributes. Many of you will know that the church did not take a mortgage to build this temple. You would also know that its construction was not financed with a big contribution from a wealthy donor. Instead, the funds were accumulated precious penny by precious penny over a period of many years. Likewise, the bricks were built over a period of many years. The same was true of the construction. Brother Si was the church elder throughout most of this period. There were contentious building committee meetings and at times he faced criticism. However, through thick and thin he led by example. There were many Sunday mornings when daybreak would find his boys at Piaye shoveling sand onto his truck to be transported to the site at which we are currently gathered. At other times they could be found mixing cement and making bricks. We may be out of practice but believe me, Brother Si's boys can make bricks.

So many of you have chosen to come here today to celebrate with us. I want you to know that the outpouring of love and affection you have bestowed upon our father and his family is an immense source of comfort to us. We anticipated that this temple would not hold all who would wish to celebrate with us today, we could not contemplate an alternative venue because in our hearts we believe that God built this temple with Brother Si as his principal agent. And so for those of you who have not found comfortable seating we beg for your indulgence.

I would be negligent if I did not highlight his pioneering role in the spread of Adventism in the South and more generally in St. Lucia. As a kid I remember the crusades he conducted in Piaye, Gertrine, Derriere Morne, La Ressource, Piero, Cacoa, Augier, and so on. I remember Sabbath visits to Victoria, Soufriere, L'Abbaye, Babonneau, Desruisseaux, Castries, Micoud, and on, and on where my dad was the featured speaker. I recall and appreciate the energy he brought to bear on his sermons, the clarity with which he explained the scriptures and his uncanny ability to totally capture his audience's attention even when he was telling stories they had heard him tell before. Brother Si sustained this effort over the course of many decades and in so doing was a builder of the church sermon by sermon, crusade by crusade, new member by new member, counseling session by counseling session, and prayer meeting by prayer meeting.

I believe that our father's work on this earth is complete. He gave his all and more. Every day he took small steps towards greatness. When he died he was a great man.

My wife Rosemary and I expect the birth of our second son in mid July. Unfortunately, he will never meet his paternal grandfather. However, we hope to ensure that he will benefit as I and so many others have benefited from having known Daddy. So in recognition of, and in homage to, the legacy of St. Brice Reynolds we are pleased to share with you our intention to name our son Bricen.

Finally, I imagine that in the moment before his passing God

*would have told Daddy, "well done, thou good and faithful servant:
enter into the joy of thy Lord."*

YES, THE MAN MY BROTHER WAS TALKING ABOUT was my father;
not the man lying in the casket, dressed as if he couldn't
make out the difference between a funeral and a wedding.
At the church service I too paid tribute to my father. I read
a poem titled, *I Remember,* I had written some years before
for Father's Day.

*I remember the diligence with which you shaped
tops that spun us into delight,
the care with which you crafted kites
that set us soaring.
I remember you bringing us
cashew nuts from your love of the land
when we were unable or unwilling to
accompany you to the farm.
I remember you deliberately leaving
food on your plate when we stared
in greed upon your supper like a hawk a prey,
waiting to pounce on the remains.
I remember your smile, pregnant with patience,
forbearance and affection, shining down upon a
little boy, otherwise lost.
I remember the hard times. The times
your sewing machine chewed away the night,
you buried in cloth trimmings,
chalk and cloth dust, and piles of cloth waiting
impatiently for your hands to fashion; and all the
while, we, without a care, oblivious to*

the bread and stone struggle you were waging
with only thread and needle as your weapon,
kept bombarding you with trifles: "Daddy, he
is calling me name," "Daddy, he is looking at me
big eye," "Daddy, he hit me first," "Daddy,
he stole my marbles." But still you took time
off to settle the peace, to give right
where right belonged and wrong where it belonged.
I remember those days. Those days when sleep
was a luxury you could not afford, not when
nine insatiable mouths opened with a question mark.
Yes, I remember. I remember the banana carrying days.
The days when we left home in the dark
and returned in the dark,
the days of crossing raging rivers,
climbing hills, descending valleys,
with our precious cargo, the family's lifeblood,
making grooves in our heads, but always returning
for yet another load, even when
our feet said "We cannot take another step,"
our necks said "We cannot support not even one more feather."
Hard times, yes,
but we were together, you leading the way.
Pleasant memories these hard times have become.
I remember. I remember big Christmas Day, you
sawing away, building hives for bees,
to build a nest for us. I remember.
I remember this one morning, the morning at
New Dock Beach, when the sea had done swallow
 my sister and a friend of the family
in a hole made by a boat that had come

too close to shore, and you, with no hesitation,
searched the bottom of the ocean for what
to me were many lifetimes and brought up the
friend of the family and then my sister,
like Lazarus from the grave; if you had
hesitated for one moment, the sea
would have claimed them forever.
Yes, I remember. I remember that day we were
fishing on The Dock, when a friend asked you,
"Would you give your life to save any of
your children?" and before you had answered
"Of course," I already knew the answer,
because I remembered the morning on New Dock Beach,
the morning, if not for you, my sister
would not have returned like Lazarus from the grave,
or Jonah from the fish's belly.
Yes, I remember, especially on Father's Day,
the small things, the small things that tell it all,
that account for all of me.
I remember.

YES, THE MAN THE POEM IS TALKING ABOUT is my father, not the man lying there in the church, for when in church my father didn't lie down. Yes, he preached; yes, he sang praises; yes, he kneeled and prayed; but never did he lie down, and definitely not in a vampire box.

The reading of the poem took everything I had inside of me, or maybe it had taken everything I had inside of me to read the poem. Either way the reading emptied me out; emotionally I had nothing left. After the reading, when on trembling legs I took my seat, I couldn't hold back any longer. I sobbed. Afterwards people said I was very brave to have read the poem. But I didn't see it as bravery. It needed to be done. It was the least I could do for my father, for the family, and for the hundreds who had come to pay their respects and support the family. I have no doubt my brother who read the eulogy saw it that way too.

People said it was a great funeral, they liked that it was more a celebration of my father's life than the mourning of his death. Like in true African fashion where in some cultures births are occasions for circumspection because people know not what the child will bring to the world and deaths are occasions for celebration because the life is known. I don't recall that we had consciously planned it that way. I suspect it came out that way, assuming the people were right, because this was how we felt about our father, indeed his was a life worthy of celebration.

THE NIGHT BEFORE THE FUNERAL, the young man who killed my father came to say he was sorry. But what is he sorry about? Is he sorry that my father is dead? Is he sorry because he was the one who killed my father? Is he sorry because he fears the consequences that will follow the death of my father? To have spun off the road, hit another vehicle, run over my dad, and then plunge into a wall fence, the driver must have been driving recklessly indeed. Didn't he realize the road was wet so he should take it easy? Or is he one of those drivers who overtake at blind corners, on bridges, on top of hills? One of those drivers who drive at night with one headlamp? One of those drivers who curse people whom they think are driving too slowly, calling them *lanmen won* (round hand)? One of those drivers who think driving fast and recklessly is a sign of their manhood?

The driver is sorry, but does he realize that given his reckless behavior it was just a matter of time before he would kill somebody's child, somebody's brother, somebody's sister, somebody's husband, somebody's wife, somebody's mother, somebody's father? Does he realize that if he continues driving as though he has a rendezvous with death, my father's life will not be the only life he will take?

And who is this man to be taking lives? How many lives has he created? Who appointed him God?

He says he is sorry, but what good is his sorry? Where is my father? Tonight, who will take the place beside my mother that my father had occupied for over fifty years?

I want my father back. Tell the man who killed my father it is not his sorry I want. I want him to tell me where he has taken my father hostage. For I want to take my father at least one more time to see his bees. And on behalf of all the families out there who have had their loved ones snatched by reckless drivers, I would like to ask those drivers where are they holding those people hostage, because their families would like to take at least one more walk with them.

THROUGHOUT THE FUNERAL AND BURIAL PROCESSIONS and throughout the wake and other activities that followed the death of my father, I stayed close to my mother. I had the distinct feeling I was part of a mafia or mobster family whose head or Godfather — my father — had been gunned down, and the family could not afford, could not survive, the death of the second in charge — my mother. So I stayed close to my mother, guarding her as if her life was in clear and imminent danger.

I could have never anticipated feeling that way, and I don't know why I felt that way, for my family was the opposite of a crime family. My parents were the pillars of religious and spiritual strength. But this sense of danger, this instinct to protect my mother, was my most acute, my most vivid sensation during this period of mourning.

The Value Of A Life

THRICE I WENT TO THE PRELIMINARY HEARING of my father's court case. Both times the motorist, my father's killer, came to shake my hand as if congratulating me on a deed well done, or as if to mollify me. I didn't want to shake his hand. In fact, I would have preferred never to have known him, never to have laid eyes on him. I would have preferred he remained some vague entity to which I couldn't put a face, a height, an age, a complexion, a weight, a reality. Because every time I saw him, and when, out of politeness, the same politeness my father taught me, I unwillingly shook his hand, images of my father knocked down on the side of the road like a useless paper doll with dirt in his eyes, nose, and mouth came to me. So when I saw my father's killer, I tried not to look into his eyes; and when I shook his hand, I tried not to feel it.

It was a court case that would end up nowhere. I was to

appear in court to provide an identity statement that the man killed on the morning of June 6, 2002, off the St. Jude's Highway in Vieux Fort, was indeed St. Brice Reynolds, my father—as if this fact wasn't already established—and thus for the case to be officially launched. The first two times the court was adjourned because the judge didn't show up. So it was only at my third court appearance that I was able to perform my duty of providing a statement of death. Each appearance had meant missing a day of work because Vieux Fort, where the court was held, is at the opposite end of the island where I worked. The police officers on the case were very kind and sympathetic, telling me this was a big case, a serious case, and I should hold on. But then I got wind that these same officers had been telling my father's killer that he shouldn't worry, that it was just an accident, it could have happened to anyone, so nothing much would come of it. I said to myself, "Why am I wasting my time? This is a police case, a criminal case. I have already carried out my responsibility of making the requisite statement, so why should I continue placing myself in the same room with my father's killer, laying eyes on the person whom of all the persons in the world I least wanted to see? Why am I putting myself in harm's way? Why this needless suffering? If I keep attending court when will the healing begin?" So I stopped attending court, and the killing of my father became yet another statistic in St. Lucia where the victims of crime and not the perpetrators are the ones at fault, so woe be unto those who fall victims to crime; where court cases drag on to fizzle into nothingness; and where, amazingly, in such a small place many murders go unsolved.

While all this was going on, the aunt and uncle of my father's killer, both Seventh Day Adventists and friends of the family — in fact the uncle was a bosom friend of both my dad and my eldest sister's husband — kept coming around the family in pleading and apologetic tones. I suspect to express remorse and regret on the one hand and to seek forgiveness and hence leniency for their nephew on the other. I say suspect, because I tried to avoid direct contact with them as much as I had tried to avoid contact with their murderous nephew, so I hadn't given myself the chance of finding out exactly what they were after. I could understand their predicament. They were friends of my father and his family, but they didn't have the luxury of outrage over the killing of my father because it was their very own nephew who had done the killing. So I could understand where they were coming from, but I just couldn't bring myself to entertain them, I wasn't in a forgiving or forgetting mood. In fact, up till today, as with their murderous nephew, I wouldn't mind never laying eyes on them. But out of politeness, the same politeness my father taught me, I still greet them when I run into them.

I didn't see my father on the ground reduced to a ragged, thrown away doll. I was at work in Vide Bouteille, Castries, when I got the news. And at work I was in the kitchenette about to brew coffee to start my day when the managing director, a short, red skin, accommodating and sympathetic man with a great facility for telling jokes, came to me with the message. But apparently I didn't want to hear the message, much less understand it. At first I thought he was telling me a friend of mine from Vieux Fort was in an accident. So my first thought was how come the managing director who is from the neighboring island of St. Vincent and who has never lived in Vieux Fort knows my friend? So not wanting to hear nor understand the message, or, at the very least, to delay my understanding of it, I kept asking him, "What you say? What you say?" Finally, after several attempts, my boss's message got through to me. My friend had called to say my father was in an accident. I called home. My sister, the youngest of the three girls in the family and eighteen months my senior, said, "Come home, daddy is dead."

The coffee remained unbrewed and my morning never got started. When I arrived back in Vieux Fort, my father had already been carried to St. Jude, a hospital a few hundred yards north of where my father was killed. But it would have made no difference if the hospital had been at the very spot of the accident, because, according to my mother, as soon as she saw my father's lifeless body in the dirt, she knew right away he was dead. So she did the only thing she could do for him. She removed the dirt that clung to his eyes, nose and mouth.

This was how I acquired the image of my dad discarded and abandoned by the roadside like a doll that was of no more use to a child. And it was because I didn't want to be reminded of this image that I didn't want to shake the hand of the driver who had killed my father and I would have preferred to have never laid eyes on him and to never again run into his forgiveness-seeking aunt and uncle.

THE LAST TIME I took my father to see his bees was two weeks before his death. It was a weekday and I was a bit annoyed to be called away from my own activities, but I swallowed my annoyance and dropped off my father on top of New Dock Road, at the foot of Moule-a-Chique, a peninsula marking the southernmost tip of St. Lucia and therefore Vieux Fort. His hives were scattered under the bush that clothed the hill above New Dock Road, overlooking the Caribbean Sea and the World War II American-built maritime dock or finger pier from which New Dock Road got its name.

Lately my father's bee operation had come under severe threat. At his New Dock operation someone had lifted the hut in which he extracted the honey from the honeycomb lock, stock and barrel. At La Retraite, a few miles northwest of Vieux Fort and near the village of Grace, where he also kept bees, the thief had been a bit more considerate; he lifted only the roof of galvanize. A year before my father's death, parasitic mites (*Varroa jacobsoni* or *Acarapis woodi* or both) had wiped out many of his bee hives. And those he had managed to save by the application of a pesticide, boys in nearby Shantytown-turned-Bruceville had set on fire, thrown down, and walked away with the honeycomb. After my father's death I found out there had been a honey racket. Adults in the neighborhood paid teenage boys to steal my father's honey. But despite the combined oppression of man and nature, unperturbed, my patient and long-suffering father, like a man guarding a state treasure, carried on with his bee operation.

I suspect the wholesale lifting of my father's New Dock hut was a drug dealer's retribution. My father had found a cache of cocaine hidden in the hut which he had promptly reported to the police. Cocaine finding its way to an occasionally used hut hidden under the bush not too far from the coast wasn't an unexpected occurrence, because Vieux Fort fishermen were finding cocaine on the open seas on a regular basis, and occasionally residents of Bruceville would find cocaine washed ashore on the beach. So it wasn't surprising that the bush-carpeted hills hugging the Vieux Fort coastline were awash with clandestine drug activity. My mother wasn't as intellectual as my father, but she was much less idealistic and much more shrewd, practical and suspicious when dealing with people. She was totally against my father reporting his discovery to the police, for, as she reckoned, who knows if the police are not in cahoots with the drug dealers, and who would protect my father from the wrath of these criminals? My mother was all business and vexation about the incident, but my father was adventurous or even romantic about it, an amusement to talk about, to add color to his day. The drug dealers on the other hand must have reasoned that if they couldn't use the hut then neither would my father.

As I turned around to return to my own doings, my father said I should come back for him in two hours. I returned two hours later and clambered under the bush to locate my father. I couldn't find him and by then bees were eating me up, eating me up. Not since my teenage days when my siblings and I pitched in to help my dad harvest honey, the days when I went to school with puffed up eyes, nose and lips, had I been stung by so many bees.

I was angry. "He told me to come back in two hours, so where the hell is he?" I called out to my dad and as he answered I moved in the direction of his voice. When we reached each other, he said I should go home and get his overalls. I was doubly angry. Why didn't he walk with the overalls in the first place? I bit my lips and drove home for the overalls. I reentered the bush and handed the overalls to my dad. More bees ate me up. Ate me up! I left my dad in the bush and waited for him roadside. Half an hour later he emerged with a smoker in his hand, a veil on his head and dressed in his overalls, reminding me of a space walker. Bees had stung him on every inch of his body. He said a hive fell and the bees had gotten angry. Through all the telling my father was smiling. As if he were happy the bees had finally gotten their revenge for him stealing their honey. As if justice had been served. As if now, with all the bee stings, my father would sleep more soundly knowing he had paid his debt to the bees. I was ashamed for being annoyed about having to take my seventy-eight-year-old dad to see his bees. I was doubly ashamed for being angry at him. I was ashamed of my ungratefulness. After all, it was this very bee operation that had helped clothe, feed, and educate me.

I CAN NEVER BE THE MAN MY DAD WAS.

I WENT TO THE PLACE, the tomb, where they had buried the man who was passing as my father. I placed flowers on the tomb as I had seen done so many times in movies, especially mafia movies, hoping (wishing, rather), the man they had entombed there would rise like Lazarus or Christ from the grave, or Jonah from the fish's belly, to tell me where my father, the humble farmer, tailor, preacher, and beekeeper, was being held hostage. Nothing happened except tears flowing down my face.

THE ADJUSTER for the driver's insurance company told me that other than reimbursement for burial and wake expenses there wasn't much compensation to be had for the wrongful death of my father. My Dad had been old and retired, he said. Meaning, because of my father's age and income, he wasn't worth much. I wondered why the adjuster didn't tell that to the many heads of state around the world who had long left seventy behind, or to my oldest brother, to whom my father was best friend and principal business advisor, or to my mother, to whom my dad had been constant companion for over half a century, or to the fifty-five-year-old man who told me, tears in his eyes, how my dad had been more of a dad to him than his own dad ever was?

OF WHAT VALUE IS A LIFE? Is the value of a life the present value of the life's income stream? Should the value of a life be measured in terms of years, deeds, income generating capacity, or in terms of the usefulness of the life to others? The adjuster told me my father had already passed the nation's average life expectancy. Meaning that, statistically, my father was dead long before he was killed. Meaning that my father had been a living dead for quite some time — eight years to be exact. So in truth and in fact my father's worth ought to be valued at zero. Upon hearing this, I thought: "So it was quite okay for someone to run off the road and transform my father into a useless, dirty, paper doll. After all, how can you murder someone who is already dead? Or, what else can you do with something that is worth nothing than dispose of it in the garbage dump?" I thought, "Why don't we gather together all the elderly and gas them in a gas chamber, like Hitler did the Jews?"

To the adjuster and the insurance company, my father may have been worthless. To the reckless twenty-four-year-old driver, my father may have been dead before he killed him. But don't tell this to my mother; don't tell this to my eight brothers and sisters; don't tell this to me; don't tell this to his Seventh Day Adventist flock whom he shepherded; don't tell this to the hundreds of people who attended his funeral; don't tell this to the many more who depended on him for love, direction and guidance. Worthless or not, I want my father back.

MY FATHER HAD A PREMONITION ABOUT HIS DEATH. A few weeks before the accident, my eldest sister and her husband were going to America on vacation. My sister wanted my mother to come along. My mother loves traveling so she wanted to accept the invitation. Besides, she and my eldest sister are like two sisters; their homes are side by side in the same yard and operate like one household. But my father objected. There was no question of him going because he didn't want to die on a plane or in some foreign country. Neither did he want my mother to go, because, as he said to her, "You might return to a dead husband." My mother didn't go. How could she after my father had put it in those terms? So it wasn't my mother who returned home to a dead husband. It was my sister who returned home to a dead father.

My father may have had a premonition about his death, but he wasn't afraid to die. He was more concerned about things being in order before he passed away. He wanted to make sure his children and grandchildren got on okay in the world after he was no longer in it. So convinced was my father of his imminent death, that death met him in the midst of having his farm land at Grace surveyed, to, as he said, avoid his children having trouble claiming the property after he was gone. This was the only business my father had left

unfinished. Still, that was no fault of his. He had been working on getting the survey done for more than a year, but the
surveyor, who was based in Castries, an hour's drive away,
kept postponing.

The Story Of My Father

ONCE MY FATHER ASKED, "Have I told you how my nephew nearly killed me?"

"No," I replied.

He said, "Can you keep a secret?"

"I think so."

"Are you sure? Don't tell me you can and next thing you can't."

"Yes, Daddy, I can keep a secret."

It was a weekday afternoon and we were seated in the balcony of my parents' home, with a clear view of St. Jude's Highway and its constant traffic, and surrounded by my mother's garden interspersed with banana plants, coconut palms, and plum, sour sop, mango, golden apple, cashew and guava trees. Raised in the inland and rural hamlet of Desruisseaux, seven miles northwest of Vieux Fort, my mother had transported the farm to her yard. Her love of gardening knew no bounds. Every square inch of the yard not taken up by drains and foot paths was under cultivation, and, making sure nothing went to waste, the strip of land between her fence and the public road was also put to good use.

My father said it happened before he went to England, when he had a tailor shop on Clarke Street, the street running through the center of Vieux Fort.

He said, "It's a long story, but for you to understand what happened I will have to start with my mother."

He said that his mother had been a cultural and spiritual icon. She played a key role in cultural and Roman Catholic religious ceremonies. She was an active member of the La Rose society, helped to christen children, and officiated at Roman Catholic First Communion rites. For most of those ceremonies and celebrations his mother dressed in a manner befitting a priestess. Sometimes she wore a *wob dwiette*, a grand robe worn by French colonials from which the Madras, St. Lucia's national dress, is derived. Other times she was dressed in fine white linen or cotton. But always she was decked out in gold and silver jewelry — earrings, necklaces, bracelets, rings — which were a legacy of the island's French Creole culture and an integral part of the mode of dress at the time. When my father was describing his mother, the person who came to mind was none other than St. Lucia's queen of folk, the late Dame Marie Selipha Sessene Descartes.

My father said that his parents had separated when he was no older than ten. He didn't explain why they separated, and at the time I didn't ask. After the breakup, his mother left Bellevue, a hinterland of Vieux Fort, with her eldest daughter and moved to the Mabouya Valley, in the

district of Dennery, midway between Vieux Fort and Castries, leaving behind her husband, her two sons and two
daughters. The daughter his mother took with her was of a
different father to my dad and apparently her favorite child.

This was a difficult time for my father. Besides the agony
of being separated from his mother, occupied with farming,
rearing animals and earning a living, his father could ill afford the time to look after him and his other siblings, so the
burden of cooking and housekeeping fell on my father's second eldest sister, who was only a few years older than him.
My father's sister became his de facto mother, which probably explains the close bond between them that lasted their
lifetime.

Several years later my grandparents made up, and the
family was reunited in the Mabouya Valley. By then my
dad's father, who loved animals, had acquired quite a few
goats, sheep, and cattle. Rather than herd the animals the
thirty miles or so from Bellevue to the Mabouya Valley, he
sold them.

Sugar was still king in St. Lucia, and as home to one of
the few remaining sugar factories on the island, from an employment standpoint, the Mabouya Valley (also one of the
largest sugar cultivation areas), was an attractive place to
live.

However, a few years after the move to the Mabouya
Valley, tragedy struck. My dad's father, who was in his mid-
forties, fell ill and passed away. My dad said the one thing
his father left him was a calf. My dad treasured that calf. He
cared for it even more than he cared for himself. He had inherited his father's love of animals. He took great pleasure
and satisfaction watching the calf that was his father's final

gift to him grow into a fat, beautiful heifer. But as if this was too good to be true, his eldest sister, his mother's favorite child, now married, appropriated the heifer and gave it to someone as *dimotyé*. By this transaction the ownership of the cow was effectively transferred to a new owner who continued to rear the animal, with my father's sister gaining a half-share interest. People usually gave their animals *dimotyé* when they had neither the interest nor the time to take care of them. My father said he didn't make much fuss over this misdeed, but it had really pained him to see the only thing his father had left him discharged to a stranger. After all, he had the time, he was more than interested in taking care of the animal, and he was doing a good job of it. So clearly his sister giving the heifer away as *dimotyé* was simply a ploy to lay claim to it. As my father was relating the story, I got the distinct feeling that to him losing the heifer had been like losing his own father all over again. Of course, to be honest, this was the story of my father's life. Someone, some entity, was always doing him wrong, but for the sake of keeping the peace he let the injurious deed slide. So as my father was relating his story, I wondered, not for the first time, why he didn't put people in their place, why he hadn't protested and blocked his sister's indiscretion?

But by then I was too enrapt in the story to interrupt with questions. I was no longer conscious of the din of the traffic on the St. Jude's Highway. The gentle, caressing breeze blowing across the balcony that would normally cause drowsiness had no such effect on me.

My father said at around that same time his mother took some of the money his father had saved from the sale of his animals and bought a plot of land in Vieux Fort on which she helped build a house for the same daughter who had denied my father his cow.

It was the time of the Americans. World War II was raging. The Americans had transformed Vieux Fort into a military base, so the once sleepy, fishing and sugarcane factory town was booming; jobs were plentiful, and housing was in short supply. Having just turned eighteen, my father too tried his luck in Vieux Fort. But he didn't find employment with the Americans. He said that in those days few people could read and write, and many couldn't speak English. As my father was one of the few who were literate, a gang of men followed him when he went to the Americans in search of employment. In asking for work my father ended up acting as the representative of the group. Apprehensive of any semblance of organized labor, the Americans asked my father who appointed him spokesman, and they hired everyone but him. So instead of getting his share of the American easy money, my father learned tailoring, and by the time the Americans left (shortly after the 1948 Fire that destroyed Castries City), leaving behind a wealth of infrastructure but a dependency syndrome that some say still lingers in Vieux Fort, my father had become a well-established tailor.

My father got married at the age of twenty six. Soon after his mother died and left behind a trunk filled with fine linen and jewelry. But it was with my father she left the keys to the trunk. He was the only one she trusted to do the right thing and see the stuff was shared evenly among her children. Somehow the trunk ended up in the home of my father's eldest sister. She and her husband begged my father for the keys, but he refused to give it to them because according to him all his brothers and sisters needed to be present when the trunk was opened. My father said that when the time came to open the trunk, to his great surprise, it was empty. He said to this day he couldn't figure out how his sister and her husband had gotten to the contents of the locked trunk.

But, before long, some of the items from the trunk — jewelry, especially — started to appear around town. It was from his landlord my father first caught wind that his nephew, his eldest sister's first child, was on the market with his mother's jewelry. When my father's nephew approached the landlord with a gold chain, recognizing the jewelry as belonging to my father's mother, he took the chain under the pretext he would pay for it later and gave it to my father. Since the chain was likely to be the only thing my father would own out of everything his mother had left behind, he kept it. It was this chain that nearly cost my father his life.

My father said, "The day my nephew came after me with a knife I was in my tailor shop. Luckily my landlord had already sent word my nephew was coming. I sat with my back facing the door of the shop and placed a mirror in front of me so I would get a glimpse of anyone entering. When I saw my nephew appear with a large butcher knife, I didn't panic. I was ready. I waited. He rushed in but as he raised his arm to plunge the knife into my back, I turned around and caught his arm at the wrist. In those days I was very fit and very strong in my arms. I used to run on the beach on mornings and do up to a hundred pushups. When I tell you I was strong in my arms, I was really strong.

"I caught his wrist, stood up and twisted his arm behind his back. The knife fell to the floor. This was how my nephew, the son of my eldest sister, nearly killed me."

My father had escaped the murderous hands of his nephew only to be mowed down by a reckless, god-playing motorist fifty years later.

This story of my cousin's attempt on my father's life was shocking enough, but what shocked me even more was what happened afterwards.

My father said that this same nephew had been getting into so much trouble that his parents were worried he would soon end up in jail. Before it came to that they wanted to send him away to England. But despite the benefit of most of the trunk's valuables, they didn't have the money to pay for their son's passage. So it was my father who paid half the fare for the nephew who just a few months before had tried to murder him for a mere gold chain.

Why do I recount this story, even though I had promised my father that I would never repeat it? I relate this story to say I can never be the man my father was. I don't have it in me to forgive a nephew, a cousin, a brother, a sister, a mother, a father, who tried to kill me, certainly not to the extent of paying their passage to get them out of trouble. Yes, once the danger has passed, I could probably refrain from retaliation. But actively help my would-be-murderer? No. I don't have this kind of magnanimity, I don't have such a big heart, I cannot raise myself to this level of compassion, to this level of greatness. Therefore, I can never be the man my father was. Come to think of it, knowing my father, he has probably already forgiven the motorist who sent him to his grave.

This same nephew, yes the one who had made an attempt on my father's life, came to my father's funeral. At the wake he said to me, "Why you all eh coming and visit me?"

I smiled politely but didn't provide him an answer. But to myself, I said, "You tried to kill the man and now you want his children to visit you. For what? To give you an opportunity to finish the job you had started on their father?" Clearly, my cousin had made a miscalculation. He didn't realize I hadn't inherited my father's spirit of forgiveness; I am not and could never be as big a man as my father.

This incident with his nephew was probably the only attempt that had been made on my father's life. But, as hinted above, the gist or portrayal of the story wasn't an aberration. It seems to me the story of my father has been the story of people taking advantage of him and getting away with it. My father's limited recounting of his life is replete with incidents of people taking advantage of him. And during the period of my growing up, be it the laborers working on his farm who in his absence worked just a couple hours for a full days pay; or the personnel of the St. Lucia Banana Growers Association (SLBGA) for whom he transported bananas, who at his expense gave preference to other truckers in the loading queue; or his tailoring clients who refused to pay him for work more often than not he had spent sleepless nights completing; someone was always taking advantage of, or abusing, my father. And it seemed that always the story would end with my father acknowledging he was being abused but choosing to turn a blind eye or not retaliating. He would say something like, "I know they were doing me wrong, but for the sake of peace I left it alone."

Of course, that was my impression as a child. Now as an adult I realize it is impossible to go through life without someone occasionally rubbing you up the wrong way or perceiving you have wronged them. So am I making more out of my father's complaints than he meant to convey? Or was my father a sensitive person who read more into situations than what the facts suggested? Or did my father suffer from a victim mentality in that when he saw trouble coming he would do nothing to deflect it, yet would complain afterwards of being a victim? It may be a bit of all the above, but when I weigh in the impressions of my siblings on the matter and my mother's constant nagging of my father for tolerating people taking advantage of him and for him putting the interest of others before his, I would have to conclude that in both his personal and business dealings my father more often than not was left holding the short end of the stick.

People said my father was too soft, he had too good a heart. Is that a compliment, or is that an insult? Was my father just a weak man? Didn't he realize people took advantage of him because they knew he had a history of not retaliating, of letting things slide? Did just one look at his demeanor tell people this was a man they could have their way with? In brief, one way or the other, did people know there would be no cost to violating my father's rights?

What do I know for sure? I know my father had a kind, loving heart. He hated to see people suffer, to see people being taken advantage of. My father's youngest sister was special, she was what St. Lucians called retarded or *moumou*, or, more correctly, *gorgor*. The strongest memory I have of this aunt had to do with my father's reaction to a man who was trying to befriend her. My father was very angry about the man attempting to take advantage of his sister, and made it clear to the would-be-lover that if he wouldn't leave his sister alone, he was quite prepared to beat sense into him. My father vented about this situation as if a great evil, a great injustice was being done to his sister. As a preteen I didn't quite understand why all the fuss, and why should someone miss out on the pleasures of this life just because they were retarded? But what I did understand, loud and clear, was that my father loved his family and he would go to great lengths to protect them, and while he may tolerate people taking advantage of him, he sure wasn't going to stand by and let them take advantage of his loved ones. Clearly, my father was a Hector, a humble hero.

My father always rooted for the underdog. In Desert Storm he happily sided with Iraq, in the Palestinian-Israeli conflict he sided with the Palestinians. The government privatizes an industry, my father commiserates with the workers who stand to lose their jobs, considering it a great injustice. When, using a bit of my economics training, I explained that the private sector would run the operation more efficiently than the government, the displaced workers would find jobs in other sectors, and in the long run the country may be better off with privatization, he would answer, "How about the people who have their families to feed?" My father would come up with elaborate theories in defense of the underdog. Theories whose logic I sometimes couldn't quite follow. So most times I just sat there and listened to him. My father sided with the underdog, he could relate to the underdog, it seemed he saw himself as an underdog, a long-sufferer.

I also know my father was no coward. My father said that in his youth, when a gang of guys were harassing him, trying to pick a fight with him, he would size up the group and select their leader, the biggest and strongest of the lot, and take the fight to him. He would beat him up badly, and thereafter that gang would never trouble him. To me this is an act of bravery. To consciously choose to fight the very person who has the best chance of beating you is nothing less than a Clint Eastwood, a John Wayne, a Jason Statham kind of bravery. My father was a hero. My father was a brave man. He tolerated people taking advantage of him not because he was afraid to stand up for himself or for his ideas and opinions, but because he placed a high price on his peace of mind, on keeping the peace.

I'm much less tolerant than my dad of people taking advantage of me. But I cannot call myself brave. Neither can I call myself a hero. In my whole life I have had fewer than three fights, and there was never any conscious effort on my part to initiate the fighting. In fact, I went to great lengths to avoid a fight, and fought only because there was no escape, because I had no choice, because punches were being thrown at me. So you could hardly call my response fighting back or an act of bravery. But my father who displayed a John Waynian or Clint Eastwardian type of bravery had much more compassion than me. That's why I know I can never be the man he was.

IT WAS AT THE AGE OF FIVE at the Belvedere Infant School in Vieux Fort that I first discovered just how much of a coward I was. On a Monday morning before the start of classes, one of the school's bullies could find nothing better to do than to pull on my youngest sister's hair and taunt her about its shortness. This is the same sister who, in time, was the one to tell me: "Daddy is dead, come home." She was having none of the bully's antics. Unlike me, who would display great feats of tolerance to avoid a fight, she had no qualms about fighting. Besides, she was as strong or stronger than most boys her age. In her fights with my brother who was her immediate senior, it was never clear who got the better of whom. Frankly, to the dismay of my brothers and I, my sister was a tomboy. She was ever so willing to join us in a game of cricket or soccer. But she was very aggressive and never accepted defeat. In playing cricket, nothing short of completely knocking down the wickets would convince her she was out. Plenty of playing time was wasted in trying to convince my sister of the obvious.

My sister warned the boy, but he did not take heed. My sister only warns once. Suddenly, she lunged her attack, nails and fist meeting flesh. The boy, taken completely by surprise, jumped back, howling in pain. But since fighting was his pastime, he wasted no time in the counterattack. Besides, he saw an advantage — a girl. The boy grabbed my sister at the shoulders, placed one leg across the back of her legs, and threw her to the ground. Next, he tried to pin her down. She kicked and screamed in rage. They rolled over a few times, their uniforms losing glory. As the fight progressed, despite my sister's gallant efforts, the boy was getting the better of her.

While my sister was fighting for her life and honor, I, who was only a year and a few months younger than her, stood motionless on the edge of the crowd of children who had gathered to enjoy the spectacle. Each time the boy fired a punch, the crowd chorused, "Hegas!" I overheard one girl saying, "Look her brother there, he eh lifting a finger to help his sister."

She was right. I just stood there — numb — like Peter denying he was a disciple of Christ. I couldn't lift a finger even if my life had depended on it. Still, the strangest thing was that during the fight no anger swelled up in me, and it never occurred to me I should pitch in. It was as if my sister were a stranger getting beaten by another stranger. This incident has remained the single most shameful experience of my life. To this day each time this scene replays in my head I cringe in shame. And I don't remember my sister ever mentioning that fight to anyone, neither can I recall ever talking to her or anyone else about it. Of course, my sister couldn't come home talking about being in a fight because this would invite a beating from my mother. And in my case, talking about it would have exposed myself to even greater shame. So it seems both of us had reasons to remain mute on that incident. But now I wonder what my sister had thought of me for not coming to her aid.

I MAY BE A COWARD, but my dad who was the opposite of a coward had much more compassion than me. That's why I know I can never be the man he was.

It took a long time for my dad to beat any of us. Unlike my mother, where the punishment was swift and immediate, my father did his best to avoid beating us. He would warn you once, give you a lecture as to why he doesn't want you to do whatever you are doing that's displeasing to him. He would warn you a second, third, fourth time, until finally when he couldn't take it any longer, he would tell you, "I'm tired of warning you, but you are not listening, I will have to beat." When my father said this, you could sense it really pained him to have to beat you, that he wished there was another way, but you have left him with no choice. It were as if my father disliked beating us so much that he had to say those things to work up his courage.

I dreaded my father's lectures much more than I did his beatings. In his lectures his voice was so full of love and compassion, so full of hurt and disappointment, that they were more painful to me than his beatings. After the beating you could sense my father's remorse, you could sense he had taken no pleasure in it, as if he would like nothing better than to take back the beating. In contrast, my mom would continue quarreling long after she had given you a beating, as if she wished the beating had lasted longer and had been more severe, as if she couldn't wait for the next time, as if she were willing you, "Go ahead, make my day."

As children, when our father was eating his meals, no matter that we had already eaten ours, we hanged around the dinner table and no sooner he was through eating we would rush in and pounce on the remains of his meal. We were like a pack of hyenas fighting over spoils. Sometimes our rush was premature; our hands would be in our father's plate before he was done eating. I'm not sure whether our father was playing a game with us, acting as if he were finished only to put the brakes on our rush. Through it all my father's face gave nothing away. It showed no signs of annoyance, no signs we were doing something wrong. He just sat there eating quietly and patiently, ignoring us, even, silently accepting of our misbehavior as if that was the most natural of conduct. In fact, I'm convinced that in order not to disappoint us our father deliberately left food on his plate. I suspect our father indulged us because he took pity on us, he felt sorry for us. This was the kind of father we had, and therefore I can never be as big a man as my father.

My Father's Wish

SEVERAL YEARS BEFORE MY FATHER DIED, while I was home on vacation, I took him to see his farm at Grace, another hinterland of Vieux Fort. By then he no longer drove. From St. Jude's Highway, we turned left onto the road running through La Ressource, a suburb of Vieux Fort, bypassing first the Vieux Fort Comprehensive Secondary School, the largest secondary school on the island and where I attended the last two years of secondary school, and then the Plain View School where I obtained my elementary education. When I attended these schools, some thirty years before the death of my father, La Ressource and the adjoining area of Derrière Morne were rightly considered rural. The area was sparsely populated and interspersed with cultivation and bush. But by the time of my father's death it had become a densely populated suburb.

After passing the schools, we came upon one of two bridges built by the Americans during World War Two, when they changed the path of the Vieux Fort River to flow more westerly to make room for an airforce base. We turned left after crossing the bridge, then another left onto the road that runs through Beausejour, a government operated live-stock farm. As cadets attending Union Agricultural School in the north of Castries, Beausejour was one of the farms we visited for animal husbandry training.

As we drove alongside the farm, we were greeted by the powerful scent of animal dung and grass and the sound and sight of cows in the pasture. On trips to my father's estate, this pasture aroma always represented for me the point where the town ended and the country began.

Soon after we left Beausejour behind, I said, "Daddy, what would you have studied if you had the chance to go to university?"

He said, "I'm not sure, but most likely it would have been medicine."

MY FATHER had wanted to save lives, yet all of a sudden someone took his life in the most violent of ways.

I ASKED HIM THE QUESTION, but before he had answered I already knew the answer, because since childhood I have known that my father wanted one of his children to be a medical doctor. So badly had my father wanted one of us to be a medical doctor that he named me after his doctor in England.

In fact, in all the time I have known my dad, I have only heard him express two wishes. First, he wanted at least one of his children to be a medical doctor. And second, before he died he wanted, even if for one day, to have all his children with him under the same roof. You see, by the time my father entered his sixties most of his children were scattered across the United States. My father got his second wish three years before his death when, in the summer of 1999, all his children came home to celebrate his and my mom's fiftieth wedding anniversary. He got his first wish double, but not really. To date two of his children are doctors, but they are not doctors of medicine, they are doctors of economics.

In one of my father's sermons, a poor, hard-working man sacrificed a great deal to educate his son. Shabbily dressed, out of place, but proud of his son and in good spirits, the father attended his son's college graduation ceremony. In sharp contrast to this father, the other parents attending their children's graduation were impressively dressed and obviously of some means. The son graduated with honors and at the top of his class, and was chosen to give the valediction. In his speech he thanked his teachers, some of his classmates, and even some of his classmates' parents for admonishing him and helping him along the way, but not once did he mention his father. It was as if his father never existed. After the graduation ceremony, so ashamed and embarrassed was the son of his father's lowly status, that when the father, all in smiles, walked towards him to congratulate him and to share in his glory, he turned his back and walked away.

A few months after his graduation the son declared there was no God. And no amount of preaching from his father and pastor could convince him otherwise. To the father, his son's declaration was like the dropping of a bombshell, and it hurt him even more than when the son had disowned him at the graduation, for the humble father reckoned that given how shabby he looked compared to the other parents, he could well understand how the son might be embarrassed of his father. Furthermore, the father was very pleased to see how his son had mingled so easily among the educated and the rich and famous, how his son looked no different than them. He had succeeded beyond his wildest dreams in giving his son what he never had and could never have. But to deny the existence of God the almighty, the One who had made it all possible, even down to imbuing his son with the brains to excel in higher education, was an inexcusable abomination.

Understandably, the humble father was despondent. Yet he didn't, couldn't blame his son. He took all the blame. He had failed his son and God. He had spoiled his son, focusing more on his education and the things of the world than teaching him the ways of God and salvation. He had placed his son and his son's education above God and the teachings of God. He had loved his son more than he loved God. His son had become his God. In a way he was guilty of idolatry. He worshiped his son. He had helped put his son in a position where the world was at his son's feet, but in so doing he may have caused his son to lose his soul.

However, it so happened that many years later when the son was visiting the Middle East (it may have been Saudi Arabia or Jordan or Syria, and he may have gone there on business or on vacation, I don't quite remember), he came face to face with an oilfield arising from oil gushing from a hillside. The oilfield juggled his memory to the book of Job where Job had fallen upon hard times, so much so that three of his best friends came to mourn and comfort him. In contemplating the nature of God and in questioning how God could have allowed such pain and suffering as had befallen Job, a famous discourse ensued among the four men. In this discourse, to show how low he had fallen and how exalted he once had been, Job (Job 29: 6-9) said: *When the counsel of God was over my tent; When the Almighty was yet with me, ...My steps were bathed with cream, And the rock poured out rivers of oil for me!*

Upon recalling the Bible quote, the son fell on his knees and wept. For to him, and according to my father, this was fireproof evidence that God does exist, and that the Bible is the true word of God. For right there in front of his own two eyes was the word of God in full manifestation. The son wept. Not just for his denial of God but also for the awful way in which he had treated his father, knowing how much his father had sacrificed for him, the father who had showed him the right path, the path of righteousness, which he had rejected.

I don't remember the time period in which this story took place, nor where my father first caught wind of it. I suspect he discovered the story during his stay in England. I don't remember whether at the point of the son's Middle East epiphany his father was still alive to afford him an opportunity to seek forgiveness, and I don't quite remember the role of the story in my father's sermon, whether it was about proving there is a God, or the Bible is the word of God, or to make the point that oftentimes things like money and education become a curse that makes people forsake God. But when my father was telling this story, though still a child, I always took it as a warning to us his children, and I always said to myself I must never behave towards my father and mother like this son, I must never forget my parents, I must always take care of my parents. If I were to graduate from college, I must make sure I'm proud and appreciative of my parents and I must gladly welcome them to my graduation.

My brother and I graduated with doctoral degrees two weeks apart. Understandably, given my father's sermon, it was a relief to me that he was able to attend our graduations. So one week my father honored me as he watched me accept my certificate of Doctor of Philosophy degree at the University of Florida, Gainesville, where (if I remember correctly) I was one of only two black candidates to receive a PhD; and in the next week he proudly witnessed my brother receiving his Doctor of Philosophy degree certificate at Louisiana State University in Baton Rouge, where my brother was the only black candidate to receive a PhD that day. So at the graduation ceremonies of two flagship American state universities, my father's sons accounted for two of the three PhD's conferred on black graduates. I was proud of my father, and I believe he was proud of us.

My father was good at school and he loved school. Yet he didn't attend university, neither did he attend secondary school. In fact, he didn't even have a full primary school education. His formal education was aborted at standard four when his father died. His education, however, went far beyond primary school because for the most part he was a self-educated man.

He explained how he diligently bought and read newspapers, his dictionary beside him, looking up every word he didn't know. How he unfailingly listened to the BBC to improve his pronunciation and increase his knowledge of the world. He said his English was so good and he debated so eloquently and convincingly that in England when people heard him speak, they would mistake him for his younger brother who was there studying law.

I could picture my father, him among a group of people all with more formal education than him, yet it is his words they are hanging on to as he deliberates on world events.

I can attest to my father's newspaper reading habit. Every Saturday evening as soon as the sun sets, signaling the end of Sabbath, like clockwork, he would send one of us to buy *The Voice*, the island's oldest and most widely read newspaper at the time. This habit must have rubbed off on me because up till today I continue buying newspapers whether or not I can find time to read them. These days you can get the news via the written word, the spoken word (radio) and the visual word (television and online video clips), but I still prefer the written word; I place more trust in it, and it is usually more nuanced.

No doubt reading newspapers and listening to the BBC would improve one's English and knowledge. But I think my father failed to mention another great influence on his education—the Bible and his religion. My father was a Seventh Day Adventist and as such a student of the Bible. In fact, one cannot be a serious Adventist and not be a Bible student. The Adventists divide the year into quarters and for each quarter they have a book or booklet called a Quarterly. The Quarterly is divided into weeks and for each week there is a Bible topic, which is divided into lessons, one for each day of the week. On Saturdays, during the morning Sabbath service, the congregation separates into age groups—Primaries, Juniors and Seniors—each with its own Quarterly. In these morning sessions the church becomes a babble of voices as each age group argues, discusses, expounds on the Bible topic they had spent part of each day of the week, lesson by lesson, studying. On top of these mandatory Bible lessons, the church has Bible reading plans that, if followed, ensure that its members have read the Bible end to end. And, of course, those like my dad, the Bible students among the Bible students, needed no reading or daily lesson plans to dig into their Bible. For preaching, leading the church, leading prayer meetings, leading crusades, required nothing less. This studying, interpreting, deciphering, and teaching of the Scriptures developed and sharpened my father's intellect and uplifted his writing and speech far beyond what his formal schooling would have suggested. After all, some have argued that one reason the Jews have contributed more than their fair share of world intellectual output is that the memorizing and deciphering of religious texts from an early age disciplined and developed their intellect.

My father was greatly fascinated by the Jews. In his sermon espousing the value and validity of the Seventh Day Sabbath — *There remaineth a rest for the people of God* — he would spend plenty of time explaining that one reason for the Jews' financial success was that they kept the Seventh Day Sabbath. In fact, based on my father's favorable portrayal of the Jews, I grew up with the impression they were beloved and held in high esteem throughout the world. It was only when I went to America at the age of twenty going on to twenty-one that I discovered people were begrudging of the Jews, and a reading of history made me realize that Jewish people have faced recurring and deep-seated resentment throughout the ages, across time and place, and that the Holocaust was a culmination of that resentment.

I had always sensed a mismatch between my father's intellect and his occupational pursuits, which included farming, beekeeping, tailoring, and trucking. I have always had the impression he was meant for higher intellectual pursuits such as that of a surgeon, a university professor, a scientist. Several traits of my father suggested this. First, the way he approached his various occupations. I sensed that for activities requiring more dexterity and strength than brain power, my father brought way too much logic, intellectual reasoning and theories to bear. It was as if my father's occupations weren't providing his mind with enough food to chew on, so he ended up chewing the food one time too many. Second, my father loved to explain, loved to come up with his own theories on how things work, how the world operates. He loved to teach. He was a born teacher. It was a joy sitting with him and my mother watching the evening news, my father explaining the news to my mother, explanations filled with his own biases. One of my first thoughts about my mother in connection with my father's death was how much she would miss him during the evening news. I too miss watching the news with both my parents present. Some years after my father's death my mother stopped watching the news. She said her nerves could no longer handle the violence and murders. I wonder if a second reason for her not watching the news is that it's not the same without my father beside her.

In all my father's pursuits, the activity that came closest to providing a match for his intellect was his religion: his preaching and deciphering of scriptures. My father was well up to the task. For many in the church, when there was a dispute over the interpretation of a Bible passage, my father's explication became the final word on the matter. In fact, some trusted my father's elucidations more than those of the pastors, holders of theology degrees. So impressed was I with my father's intellect, that I have often thought my father would have made better use of higher education than I have.

My father loved school and he loved learning. But I cannot say the same about me, for I have never liked school. My first few years of school was torture, and were probably the worst years of my life. Then I cried whole days at a time, and once I got started there was nothing the nuns at my elementary school could do to placate me: not bribes of Shirley biscuits, guava jam, coconut confectionary or glasses of milk. Nothing. I *mawon lékòl* (ran away from school) at every opportunity, and hid in *vòltive hedges* (grass hedges), under houses on tall pillars and in old abandoned vehicles. It was only after some serious beatings from my mother and oldest brother that it finally stuck in my head that, like it or not, school was there to stay.

It was later, at the age of seven, when my parents enrolled me (and most of my siblings) at the Plain View School where I discovered my two great loves of soccer and the make-believe-world of story books, that school became bearable. Looking back, I can now see it was the ability of these two activities to completely take me out of my world and into a world where I was transformed into the best of me that was responsible for the deep love that I developed for them. After these discoveries, I went to school to play soccer and to borrow and read story books.

My parents didn't allow me to go on the field and play ball, and at some point my mother was burning my books because she thought they were leading me astray, they were devilish. But I couldn't be defeated. At school I played soccer during recess, during lunchtime, and during recreation. And I read my story books—Louis L'Amour, Sugar Creek Gang, Hardy Boys, what have you—at home when my mother was away and sometimes well into the wee hours of the morning under the beam of a flashlight.

Somehow, despite my dislike of school, I graduated from secondary school, having done just well enough (no more, no less) to move on to the next stage. I still wasn't in love with school, but by then thoughts of career, thoughts of my future, were pressing upon me, pushing me in the direction of school. It seemed school and I had a rendezvous.

So at eighteen, after I got fired as a lab technician from the St. Lucia Central Water Authority for talking back to the supervisor of the waterplant where I worked and refusing to follow his orders, I enrolled at the Union School of Agriculture, on the outskirts of Castries. Upon graduation the government sent me to Saskatoon, Saskatchewan, Canada's middle prairie province, to study retail meat cutting at Kelsey Institute of Applied Art and Sciences with the understanding that after graduation I would return to St. Lucia to manage a much-anticipated new abattoir. But when I returned six months later, there was no abattoir waiting for me to manage. In fact, the abattoir was built not until thirty-five years later. So instead of managing a slaughterhouse, the ministry of agriculture had me running around with a veterinarian, holding down hogs for castration and steadying cows for tuberculosis shots. Hardly the kind of work to have me return to after six months of braving the Canadian winter.

Never had my life been so stagnant. I couldn't see where

my career was heading. I had enrolled in the agricultural school because traditionally the ministry of agriculture gave plenty of overseas scholarships and had one of the highest concentrations of college graduates of all ministries. But no scholarships to pursue a diploma or degree program were coming my way. No promotion or change in job status was foreseeable. My biggest fear was being seen to be afraid, to be a coward, but stagnation, the absence of progress, was next in line. So after a year of stagnation, of frustration, of disillusionment, of holding down cows and hogs, I started looking towards America as my way out.

In Saskatoon I had been in daily contact with students from the University of Saskatchewan, and to me, contrary to the then St. Lucian notion that only the brains among the brains could succeed at university, they were no smarter than me. Thus if they could pursue a university education, I had no doubt I could do the same. So I who had always hated school was now willing to cross an ocean to put myself through college.

Unlike my father who had a natural love for school, I went to school not out of love but first to avoid the whip of my mother and oldest brother, then to play sports and read story books, and then to pursue career and avoid stagnation. Thus it should have been my father and not me to have pursued higher education. Clearly, he was more deserving of it than me.

Come to think of it, my oldest brother didn't like school either, at least no more than I did. Because when he was supposed to be in school he was under vehicles learning auto mechanics. How ironic that the very person who refused to attend school, needed no excuse to put serious licks on me for skipping school. Also, growing up, I don't remember my brother ever going to church. Given my parents' twin pillars of religion and education (or should I add hard work to the list) I don't know how my oldest brother escaped both; he was a class act on "do what I say and not what I do." But the saying, *Train up a child in the way he should go, And when he is old he will not depart from it,* with which my father used to admonish his Adventist flock, must have some validity to it, because as a mature adult my brother has returned to the church.

My father was a smart man and he knew he was smart. Yet he said compared to his younger brother, the lawyer, he was nothing. He said his brother would play all day, never open a book, but when exams came he would top his class each and every time. My uncle was one of the first St. Lucian lawyers practicing with an LLB. My father was fond of him. He must have been my father's intellectual partner.

I can relate to the relationship between my father and his brother. Growing up I regarded my brother, the college professor, as smarter than me, for it seemed that with much less effort he got better grades. I am two years and two months older than him, yet as children he was able to tie his shoes long before I could, and was much better at running errands. In fact, to my great embarrassment and consternation, he was the one tying my shoes, and when I refused his offer my mother would insist I allow him the pleasure. Now I suspect it isn't so much a matter of who is smarter but that we have slightly different inclinations. Notwithstanding, since childhood we have been intellectual partners, a condition that has remained unabated.

The only time I saw my father come close to a fight was

in defense of his brother, the lawyer. It was a Sunday afternoon in Vieux Fort and my father's makeshift bus (shifted from a banana truck to a passenger bus) was loaded with passengers and set for the six mile trip to Bellevue. My uncle was already on the bus, but a man standing next to the bus who had a quarrel with him was grabbing on to him, either to start putting blows on him or at the very least to delay the bus. It didn't help that both men were intoxicated. When my father got tired of the man's mischief, in a rage he planted his feet on the man's chest and pushed him away from the bus. The man fell on his back and my father drove off. The passengers talked about the incident all along the way, saying in one way or the other my dad was a hero. But through it all my dad uttered not one word.

When we were growing up, our home was inundated with my uncle's college books; they were scattered everywhere in the house. French books, Latin books, Charles Dickens, name it, they were there. I don't know how they got there or why our home was their place of refuge, but those were the days when I devoured books, when I read just about anything. So I read my uncle's books, and when I ran out of those written in English, I started on the French and Latin ones, though I understood not a word.

AS MENTIONED EARLIER, my love affair with books started at the Plain View School, and it is a love affair that has continued unabated to this day. As an adult I visit bookstores at least five times a week, even if it is only to smell and glance at new books. One of the things I miss most about the U.S. is walking into large bookstores like Barnes & Noble, Borders, Walden, Books-A-Million, etc., taking in coffee aroma mixed with that of new books; touching, opening, thumbing books; feasting my eyes on book covers. In fact, simply being in these bookstores filled me with contentment. Some are predicting online shopping and the digital book phenomenon will soon put brick and mortar bookstores out of business. The disappearance of Borders, which up to January 2010 operated 511 superstores, may be taken as evidence of the imminent demise of bookstores. I was at a Borders in the World Trade Center the day before the 9/11 terrorist attack. I'll be one sad reader the day I can't walk in a bookstore and feast my eyes on books. I suspect the presence of my uncle's books, the sight of so many books scattered across the house, had something to do with my love affair with books. That is why when I enter a home and notice there are no bookshelves, no books scattered about, I harbor serious doubts the children of that home will aspire to higher education.

Asleep one night, before any of my books were published, but while working on *Death by Fire*, which would become my first published book, a voice asked, "What would be your greatest regret if you were to die tonight?" And to my great surprise, it wasn't that I hadn't traveled the world, or started a family, or done any of the things most people planned or hoped for, but that there wasn't even one book in any library or bookstore with my name on it. I took that as a measure of my love of books and that in pursuing writing I was on the right track and I should hurry up. From then on I promised myself that no matter what else is happening in my life, I must never stop writing.

No matter how widely one has read, books can throw up

surprises. Some years ago I was reading *Consolation*, a novel by Dr. Earl Long, a St. Lucian microbiologist living and working in the US, and was caught by surprise when the book made mention of a politician who was so confident (or wished to create that impression) of winning the elections that at political rallies he would promise the crowd that if he were to lose the elections, he would throw himself in the sea—"juboom!" You see, the book was referencing my uncle, my father's brother, the lawyer and politician. When I came across that passage, I couldn't stop laughing, for here was this writer fictionalizing my uncle's political or rather non-political career. How could I have known my uncle's political life would be the stuff novels were made of?

My uncle may have been a brilliant man but he was an unsuccessful politician and my father shared in his political failures because in the early days he helped my uncle campaign. Election after election my uncle run, but each time he lost miserably. It was after several such political defeats that he made the infamous statement of throwing himself in the sea, "juboom!" if he were to lose this next elections, thereby immortalizing his ill-fated political career. I know my uncle lost the elections, because I know he never won one, but I don't know whether he carried out his threat. Nonetheless, ever since that election he became known as "Juboom."

After each of my uncle's campaign defeats my father would gather the family around him for admonishment. It was never clear to me why he called these family assemblies and I have forgotten what exactly he said, but the impression that remained with me was that we should stay away from politics, never depend on politicians and the government, and we should stick together as a family, support each other, because when the chips are down we will have no one but each other to fall back on.

WHEN I WAS GROWING UP my father often asked, "What would you like to be when you grow up?" Looking back, these words went a long way in influencing who I have become. The question repeated often enough told me I was expected to be somebody. When I first arrived in America, I thought the Reverend Jesse Jackson-led mass action shouts of "I am somebody" was not only absurd but demeaning and embarrassing, because of course I'm somebody, and if I must go around shouting "I am somebody" to believe it, then something is terribly wrong. What I didn't realize then was that I grew up knowing I was somebody; my father's question, "What would you like to be when you grow up?" made sure of that. These magic words said not only was I somebody but great things were expected of me and I mustn't disappoint. Another thing I didn't realize at the time was that in St. Lucia and most of the other Caribbean islands, since, unlike Americans, the majority of the population was black, they didn't face the same identity issues African Americans faced. The older I was when the question was posed the more elevated the occupation I chose. To this day I still ask myself what should I be doing with my life? Am I making the most of it? Am I being of the greatest service to society? Am I doing justice to the great sacrifices my parents made to ensure I got an education? The question, "What would you like to be when you grow up?" is still begging for an answer.

FOR ALMOST TWO YEARS (May 2002 to Jan 2004) I was the senior economist at the Eastern Caribbean Telecommunications Authority (ECTEL), the advisory and policy coordinating branch of the Eastern Caribbean telecommunications regulatory regime that encompasses five countries—the four Windward Islands and St. Kitts and Nevis. Each of these countries has a National Telecommunications Regulatory Commission (NTRC), directly responsible for regulating the telecommunications sector in its territory, together forming the second branch of the telecommunications regime. The ECTEL secretariat is overseen by a board of directors with a representative from each member country. Sitting above ECTEL and the NTRCs and completing the regulatory regime is a council of telecommunications ministers, one from each member country, responsible for setting regional telecommunications regulatory policy. The Eastern Caribbean telecommunications regulatory regime was the first such multi-country regulatory regime in the world, so much so that, recognizing it could serve as a pattern for other developing countries and regions, the World Bank was heavily involved in financing its establishment.

One day, during a meeting of the ECTEL secretariat, the board of ECTEL, and the council of ministers, one particular minister, attempting to compel me to follow a certain course of action, said the ECTEL secretariat was serving at the pleasure of the council of ministers and so it was the tool of the Council. I didn't respond to the minister's remarks, but I cringed inside and said to myself, "What a travesty it would be if, after all the sacrifices my parents made to ensure I acquired an education, after the selfless life of integrity my father led, after all his admonishments of being wary of politicians, learning to stand on our own two feet, all I amounted to was a tool of politicians. A tool of the people, yes. But a tool of politicians? What a disgrace that would be, what a waste of my parents' sacrifices, what a mockery of all they stood for."

The Pursuit Of Education

IT IS SAFE TO SAY my parents, my mother especially, didn't take the education of their children lightly. And should they have faltered, my uncle the lawyer was there to make sure they stayed the course. My mother said the first thing my uncle said to her when he returned from England was that no matter what it takes or how much she must sacrifice she must send her children to school. When I was seven, my parents removed all their children from the various primary and elementary schools they were attending and enrolled them at the Plain View School, a mission school operated by the Evangelical Missionary Church and Canadian missionaries of the same faith. As mentioned before, the school was situated in La Resource, three to four miles outside of Vieux Fort. Only the two oldest children, my oldest brother and sister, escaped the Plain View School. By then my oldest brother was no longer attending school, and my oldest sister was already attending the Vieux Fort Secondary School, built by the Americans in 1962 as part of their giveback to Vieux Fort for their military occupation of the town during World War II. This American-built school was, at the time, one of only three secondary schools on the island. The other two—St. Mary's College for boys and St. Joseph's Convent for girls—were in Castries.

At that time, most schools on the island, including St. Mary's College and St. Joseph's Convent, were under the domain of the Roman Catholic Church and run by nuns and priests. This placed Adventists in a predicament because they had serious problems with Roman Catholics. To the Adventists, Roman Catholics worshiped on the wrong day of the week, bowed down to idols, prayed to the Virgin Mary, fornicated and lived in adultery, ate unclean things, smoked and consumed alcohol, and regarded the pope, a mere man, as their God on earth. In short, they were a secular, non-Christian people living in abomination; they were the Philistines and Sodom and Gomorrah of modern times. My parents were concerned their children were being contaminated with the false doctrines and paganism of the Roman Catholic Church.

On top of that, besides such Roman Catholic "nonsense" as the catechism, the making of the sign of the cross, and *Holy Mary, mother of God, pray for us ...* my parents did not feel their children were learning much of anything. Their eldest child left school barely able to read and write. Their children were discriminated against, picked on, other children were calling them *"Semdays One Week, read the Bible upside down!"* Reacting to these atrocities, their middle sons, the fourth and fifth child, besides learning nothing, were constantly getting into fights.

In search of solutions, my parents had sent them to live with my mother's cousin in Micoud, a coastal village about eight miles northeast of Vieux Fort, where they would attend the Micoud Seventh Day Adventist Primary School. But the move hadn't produced the desired results. The boys' custodians kept them so busy taking care of animals, digging yams, and carrying bananas that, always tired, they slept through the greater part of their classes. Education-wise, they were no better off at the Adventist primary school than they had been at the Vieux Fort Boys' School. In fact, from my parents' vantage point, the Micoud situation was worse. For in addition to tuition fees, they had to pay bus fare to get the boys home and back once every month, give the custodians a monthly allowance for the boys' upkeep, and each month when the boys came home, give them a hefty supply of fish and ground provisions to take back to Micoud.

Still, my parents were not enamored of the Evangelical Baptist school either, since some of their doctrines (such as the Sunday Sabbath) were at odds with Adventism. But when the Baptist pastor's wife, who lived just a few houses down the road from us, told my mother how great the Plain View School was when it came to education, and how concerned and caring the teachers were, my parents must have felt they had no choice but to take the plunge. After all, two of the things they cared most about—the salvation and education of their children—were at stake. Of course, they must have consoled themselves with: "at least, compared to the Catholics, the 'Missions' were Christians."

The Plain View School had started in 1955 with just eight students at the home of Mr. & Mrs. Harms, missionaries serving in Vieux Fort with the West Indies Evangelical Mission. Interestingly, one of the stated reasons for the Evangelical Baptists establishing their own school was because of their discomfort with Roman Catholic doctrines. Clearly, the Baptists and Adventists were strange bedfellows in the presence of a common enemy.

So in search of better education for their children while keeping their children's souls intact, my parents pulled their two middle sons, ages ten and eleven, out of the Micoud Seventh Day Adventist Primary School; their second and third daughters, ages eight and twelve, from the Vieux Fort Girls' Primary School; and their two last children (the youngest child wasn't born yet), myself and my younger brother, ages seven and five, from the Belvedere Elementary School. And off we went to the Plain View School, where, instead of nuns and priests, the school was run by Canadian missionaries; the Canadian school system replaced the British system; Canadian text books replaced British text books; Grades replaced Standards and Forms; and baseball and rounders joined cricket and football as major sports.

The move must have stressed my parents' finances to no end. Unlike the Catholic schools, which were essentially public schools, the Mission school did not come free. My parents had to spend money not only on tuition fees but also on textbooks. With seven children in school the family's education expenses must have added up quickly.

Although, thanks to my parents' hard work and industriousness and also their stint in England, we were probably a bit better off than many of our neighbors on New Dock Lane in Vieux Fort town, we were not of comfortable means by any stretch of the imagination. The wooden house we lived in had only four and a half rooms. A sitting room that served as my father's tailor shop on his return from England, a kitchen/dining room, a bedroom for my parents, another bedroom for the girls, and a space in the hallway between the girl's bedroom and the kitchen/dining room that served as the boys' bedroom. Cooking was done outside on clay coal-pots. The bath was a standpipe outside. We used pit toilets which were very difficult to construct because most of the yard was solid rock. So never deeper than a few feet, the toilet filled up quickly, forcing my father to commission a pit ever so often. In fact, digging pit toilets was a trade in and of itself. And at the time it appeared to me drunkenness was an important qualification for the job because the man who dug the pits for us (he also dug graves) was always drunk.

In time, the house was extended to include a boys' bedroom, a kitchen, and a modern toilet and bath. Also, in time, a gas stove was used alongside the coal-pot, and a washing machine replaced the hands of my mother and sisters. But in 1965, when we first enrolled at the Plain View School, these additions were still far into the future.

I could not have thanked my parents enough for the move to the Plain View School, for it was a school ideal for a child to blossom. It consisted of twelve classrooms, each with no more than twenty students. The teachers were all of the Evangelical Missionary Faith and attended the same church as most of the students and their parents, so there were close ties between the teachers and most of the parents, and the teachers treated the students as their very own. Besides, the school was fostered upon the missionary spirit. The principal was usually a missionary from southeast

Canada, namely Nova Scotia or New Brunswick. As missionaries, they were zealously dedicated to the physical, mental and spiritual health of their students. I can still recall the tear that rolled down the face of Ms. Augur, the Canadian school principal, as she predicted that soon St. Lucia would be home to a lot of vehicular traffic, and, like Canada, there would be many fatalities. With great emotional emphasis, she instilled in us dry but wide-eyed students all the necessary precautions we should take on crossing the street.

The school had ample space for a child to spread his wings. Where the cobblestone pavement at the front of the school ended, a large playing field equipped with a cricket pitch and soccer goal posts began. A large patch of guava and some tamarind trees surrounded the school grounds. At lunchtime, children gathered in family groups at their favorite spot in the bush to eat lunch. After lunch, some rushed onto the playing field to play one game or the other, including baseball, while others wandered off into the bush, frolicking around and sometimes supplementing their lunch with guava.

Half a mile away, the Vieux Fort River bordered the school on the north and east side. Along the river, mango groves flourished. On our way home from school, we often risked the ire of farmers to share in the forbidden fruits of mango trees. In the south, the school grounds were bounded by a creek which flowed into the Vieux Fort River, but dried up during the dry season. The mango trees along this creek also formed part of our orchard.

The Belvedere Elementary School was the beginning of my schooling, but the Plain View School was the beginning of my education. As I have mentioned before, it was here I discovered two of my greatest loves — books and soccer — which would change my attitude toward school and make school bearable and sometimes even enjoyable. It was at the Plain View School where, with red, blue, green, white and black square blocks of wood, under the strict discipline and dedication of Ms. Cumberbatch, I learnt the rudiments of arithmetic. It was there I discovered the world was round; there I discovered the continents and the Atlantic, Pacific, Antarctic and Indian Oceans; there I experienced for myself Greenland, the land of the midnight sun; there I visited Eskimos, with their igloos, their thick fur clothing, their harpoons and the seals and caribous they hunted for food and clothing; there I met Okafo of Ibo land and Girade of Calcutta; there I discovered the Nile, the Mississippi, and the Congo.

MY PARENTS', MY MOTHER ESPECIALLY, no nonsense attitude towards the education of their children caused my education and that of my youngest sister to take yet another turn when on September 14, 1970, three new junior secondary schools opened their doors. One in Vieux Fort, less than a hundred yards from my home, another in Micoud, and the third in the southwestern town of Soufriere, about twenty miles west of Vieux Fort. All three schools were donations of the Canadian government. During their construction and the few months before they opened for classes, the schools generated plenty of excitement among both prospective students and their parents. And who could have blamed them? Before this Canadian goodwill, there were just four secondary schools on the island — St. Mary's College, St. Joseph's Convent, the Vieux Fort Secondary School, and the Seventh Day

Adventist (SDA) Academy. It was not until a year later, in 1974, that the Castries Comprehensive Secondary School, another Canadian donation, opened its doors to become the island's fifth full-fledged secondary school. So it went without saying that these new schools were important additions to the island's education system. The schools were called junior secondary schools because they offered the first three of the five years of secondary schooling and then, subject to passing an entrance exam, students would transfer to a full fledged secondary school, such as the Vieux Fort Secondary School (renamed "Vieux Fort Senior Secondary School", to differentiate it from the junior secondary school, and later renamed "Vieux Fort Comprehensive Secondary School") to complete the last two years of their secondary education.

On a hill overlooking the Caribbean Sea, the four buildings that made up the school formed a square enclosing a small playground. Although I had sat the entrance exam for the Vieux Fort Junior Secondary School, and with great anticipation of attending I had kept a close watch on its progress, from the time bulldozers leveled off the site to the day when green chalkboards were placed in the classrooms, I almost didn't set foot in it. Luckily my parents, my mother especially, weren't about to sit idly while education passed their children by. That had already happened to their eldest child, and there was a question mark on their second eldest daughter and their two middle sons. Because by the time they had learned sufficiently at the Plain View School to stand any chance of passing the entrance exams to the Vieux Fort Secondary School, they were over the age limit. For them the Plain View School had come too late. Thus far only their eldest daughter was on her way to acquiring a secondary school education.

That was the problem with St. Lucia back then. Resources were so scarce that there were usually no second chances. To enter each stage of the education system a child had to be no more and no less than a certain age and had to take some kind of an entrance exam. Either way, if the child was over the cutoff age or failed the entrance exam, the child was doomed. There were no second chances. And, regarding the entrance exam, it wasn't a matter of failing or passing. That had nothing to do with it. The whole purpose of it was to cull out the most promising students because there was space for just so many. Now, it wasn't a question of choice of school. It was whether or not a child attended a secondary school, period.

There was a change of government in 1997, and within eight years of this new administration a sufficient number of secondary schools were built such that the education situation was completely reversed, meaning there were now more secondary school places than there were secondary school bound students, and the entrance exam was no longer about whether or not a child will attend secondary school, but which secondary school the child will attend. This made me wonder whether all along the country could have secured more secondary schools, but the government of the day had accepted limited secondary school places as the natural order of things. And I now wonder, given the multitude of overcapacity universities in Europe and America, what's preventing the government from securing enough scholarships from these universities to bring the percentage of the population with college education on par with those of developed countries? And I also wonder whether, once again, our government has resigned itself to the notion that the current state of affairs is what is possible.

Nonetheless, in 1970 when the Vieux Fort Junior Secondary School opened its doors, such rumination was probably the furthest thing from my mother's mind. Most likely what occupied her was the thought that once again education was about to pass her children by. So on the opening day of school, exam results or no results, name on roster or not, my mother sent me marching to the Vieux Fort Junior Secondary School in my brand new school uniform, as though my name was the first on the school roster.

In matters of urgency my mother had to take things into her own hands. She couldn't leave such matters to my father. Besides busy sewing, farming, transporting bananas and passengers, repairing and maintaining his truck, and preaching and conducting crusades, my father was a procrastinator. His banana plants would need propping but he would wait and wait, so by the time he finally got around to propping the bananas, many of them would have fallen, laying to waste months of previous labor. We would inform our father of needing money for a school field trip, and he may never respond, leaving us to conclude he didn't want us to go or he didn't have the money, only to dig his hand in his pocket days after the field trip has come and gone to hand over the money. Very often it took considerable nagging from my mother to get my father to replace some rotting board in the house, or to fix one thing or the other. Of course, I'm realizing I too am a procrastinator, and my youngest sister has informed me that procrastination is a common trait in men, for her husband is no different than her father in that regard. So when it came to things as important as the children's education, even though my father was just as concerned as my mother, she was the one visibly in the vanguard.

Upon my arrival, the school was swarming with children. Groups from different villages and towns were already beginning to stake their turf. There was a long line of students ahead of me waiting to register. When my turn came, the teacher, Teacher Ryan, told me my name wasn't on the roster so I should go back home, and he can't be expected to admit everyone who just walks in off the street.

I was almost in tears, but while waiting in line I had overheard the teacher asking a boy who was also from the Plain View School whether he was a good footballer. When the boy answered "yes" the teacher had registered his name. With that knowledge, rather than returning home with my tail between my legs, I told the teacher I was a very good footballer and played on the school team with the other boy from the Plain View School. The teacher smiled. Among other things, he was to be the physical education instructor for the school and therefore the soccer, cricket, and track and field coach. Knowing there would be soccer, cricket and track and field competition among the three junior secondary schools, he was keeping an eye out for athletes. He needed the best teams he could get.

"What position you play?" he asked.

"Full back," I replied.

"Yes. Yes. Aren't you Mr. Reynolds's son, the *semdays*?"

"Yes, sir."

He nodded and mumbled, "Well, Mr. Reynolds, we will see, we will see," and he wrote my name on the roster. I was in.

The school was arranged in six rooms. The least promising students were placed in Room One and the brightest in Room Six. The school did not have much information on me, but somehow they placed me in Room One, the home room of Teacher Ryan, who was also the vice principal.

When I returned home from school that afternoon with the news that the school admitted students even if they had not taken the exam or their names weren't on the roster, my mother saw a solution to a problem that must have been bothering her for quite some time. Two years before, when it was time for my youngest sister to sit entrance exams for the Vieux Fort Secondary School, she couldn't go because the exam was held on a Saturday and it was against our religion to study or write exams on the Sabbath. To my parents, everything, even education, took a second place to God. After all, He Himself said: *seek ye first the kingdom of God, and his righteousness; and all these things shall be added unto you.* To make matters worse, by the time the junior secondary schools came around, my sister had passed the cutoff age, so she wasn't allowed to sit the entrance exam.

On the second day of school, bright and early, my mother with my sister matching her stride, entered the compound of the school that promised a solution to her problem. She said that when she opened the door to the headmaster's office, he was in mid conversation with a teacher who was informing him that Room Three, her home room, was filled to the brim with students. Paying no mind to the teacher's discouraging report, my mother stood quietly at the entrance of the headmaster's office until he waved her in. She explained to the headmaster how bright her daughter was, and the only reason she hadn't taken the entrance exam was because the teachers at the Plain View School had said she was too old. But as she was coming to see the headmaster she saw plenty of students who were the same age as her daughter. This school, she told the headmaster, was her daughter's last chance of attending secondary school. To this the headmaster reportedly replied, "I will be the last one to deny someone an education. Please leave your daughter."

My mother reveled in her ability to take charge of situations and turn them to her advantage when mere mortals would have resigned themselves to their fate. She took great pride in finding the exact words at the right time to neutralize an enemy or potential enemy and to get them eating out of her hands when mere mortals would cower. And she seemed to relish even more the retelling of the story, often embellishing it to emphasize her prowess. Well, her encounter with the headmaster was just one of many such tales. She is in her late eighties, but up till today she still recounts with gusto such defining moments she encountered in her childhood and in England. She said, as a child, when neighbors were talking to her parents about her, they would identify her by saying, "the rude one."

My sister's acceptance made my mother realize how easy it was to get admitted to the junior secondary school; it must have seemed to her a free for all. I can imagine what was going through her mind. "Why not add my second youngest son to the list (by then my youngest brother, my parent's ninth and last child, had entered the picture), after all he was just as prepared as his older brother for secondary school, they were in the same class at the 'Mission' School and his grades were just as good or better than his brother's." So by the second week of the first school year of the Vieux Fort Junior Secondary School, my mother dressed my brother in the school's uniform and sent him to school like no one belonged there more than him.

Amazingly, my mother's ploy almost worked. My brother was admitted; he attended classes for two days, even answering some of the teachers' questions. But his luck ran out when the school conducted their first official, school-wide enrollment check. My brother was found out and sent home. To his great chagrin he had to return to the Plain View School while his older brother and sister moved on. I suspect being two years under the acceptance age, he was looking much too green to have gone unnoticed. To add insult to injury, a year later when it was time for my brother to sit the entrance exam to the Vieux Fort Senior Secondary School (the last year of such entrance exams, because thereafter all students would have to pass through the junior secondary schools), my brother couldn't sit the exam because it was on a Saturday, the Sabbath of the Lord. Therefore, my parents were left with little choice but to send my brother, apparently their brightest and most educationally promising child, to the SDA Academy.

My sister was placed in the prestigious Room Six and I in lowly Room One. But by the second term I was moved to Room Three, then to Room Five in my third term, and finally in my second year I joined my sister in Room Six. So in spite of my misgivings about school, Canadian generosity combined with my parents' (my mother especially) timely interventions would yet again play a key role in pushing me along the path of education.

However, it was in lowly Form One, Room One, in Teacher Ryan's history class, that I experienced the most traumatic event of all my school days, that my sense of wholesomeness was shattered, that I started to see the world through a different pair of eyes. There I learnt for the first time I was a descendant of slaves, there for the first time I learnt of the great triangle slave trade, there my education on the plight of my ancestors on the sugar plantations began. My first reaction wasn't pity for my slave ancestors, or anger at their slave masters — that would come later. My first emotion was shame. A deep, heart-wrenching shame. A shame that shattered my world, my sense of security, my sense of well-being, my sense of self-worth. A shame that my race had been subordinate to another. Now, it wasn't that there weren't any signs of St. Lucia's slave legacy. But as a twelve-year-old boy growing up in St. Lucia in the early seventies, I didn't think much of the fact that most of the women working as bank tellers had long hair and "light" skin. When I tried to chat a light skin girl and in disgust she said, *"tiwe' ko`-ou douvan mwen, ou nwe kon kaka kochon,* get away from me, you black as pig's shit," I took it she just didn't like me, and, besides, I was black in truth, blacker than most. When I heard people, especially older people, saying: "*neg mize'wab*, niggers are miserable;" "*neg mové*, niggers are bad;" "*neg modi*, niggers are cursed;" "*sé kon sa nou neg yé*, that is how we niggers are," I took it that this was just some of the things the old people say. In fact, I thought *neg* was just another name for black people. It was only nine years later, when I went to America to study, that I came to realize *neg* means nigger, one of the most derogatory words in the English language.

When people referred to government property as *"bagay bétjé*, things belonging to the white man," I reckoned this was just their way of referring to the government. Little did I know that at some level people see the government and any other authority as synonymous with their ancestors' slave masters, the white man. Yes. When people were describing someone they thought was good-looking, they would often say, "the beautiful so and so with nice skin (fair complexion) and good hair (straight hair)." But that still didn't say being black is less than being white. I had never given much thought to such foods as breadfruit, salt-fish and green figs, pork feet, cow feet, souse, all legacies of slavery, and once survival disgraces. But then what could be negative about salt-fish and green figs, delicious and all, our national dish? I had given even less thought to La Rose and La Marguerite, katumba, and our now proudly proclaimed folk music, "culture." There was nothing like Jounen Kwéyòl, or Emancipation Day celebrations (at least none I could remember) or the Folk Research Center to educate me of my roots. Besides, even if these had existed, classifying most celebrations as things of the world, entrapments of the devil, my Seventh Day Adventist religion would have made sure (as it did) I stayed as far away from my culture as possible, so I might have still remained ignorant.

In a place where both rich and poor, head of state and street janitors, teachers and pupils, managers and laborers, farmers and banana stevedores, and 97 percent of the population looked no different than me, there were no ingredients for developing any type of identity crisis or inferiority complex based on skin color. Maybe based on income and education, but not race.

Growing up in Vieux Fort I had no way of knowing that white people, or almost white people, owned the largest and most fertile estates—Roseau, Cul-de-Sac, Mabouya, and some others in Soufriere—a direct legacy of slavery. After all, the only farmers I knew were either black, Indian or *dogla* (mix of Black and Indian). I was yet to go on a school field trip to the old sugar estates to see the remnants of the sugar mills my ancestors had slaved over.

No. In a country where the few whites I saw were mostly tourists or Peace Corps volunteers, there was no white population to speak of to hint at slavery. Besides, back then, these few whites were mainly of the hippie type. In my Seventh Day Adventist's eyes they were dirty, unhealthy and immoral. They seemed to sleep with every beach bum and *wharf rat* they could lay their hands on. Since these, in the main, were the kind of white people I and my friends and probably most of the people on the island were exposed to, it was natural for me to think of my race as superior in all ways, except wealth, to the white race. And if there were any doubts of that, the Black Power Movement, the rise of Mohammed Ali, and the Rastafarian Revolution took care of that.

So unless I was told my race, a race I thought was superior to all other races, was once the slave of another race, a race I thought was far inferior to my race, the thought would have never occurred to me. And when I was told, I was devastated, my outlook on life changed forever.

GRADUATING FROM THE JUNIOR SECONDARY SCHOOL in 1973, my sister and I transferred to the Senior Secondary School for our last two years of secondary school. Two months after graduating from there, I obtained employment with the St. Lucia Central Water Authority as a laboratory technician where, after a few months of training, I was responsible for testing and monitoring water quality. It was after I was fired a year later for questioning the authority of the plant supervisor and refusing to carry out his instructions that I enrolled at the Union School of Agriculture.

Upon graduating from secondary school, my youngest sister enrolled at the Teachers Training College at the Morne Educational Complex in Castries, where she graduated with a teaching diploma. After many years of teaching, first at the Plain View School and then at the Anse Ger Secondary School, and whilst raising three young children, she enrolled with the University of the West Indies long distance learning program to pursue a degree in Counseling. The program required attending classes at the Morne. So while still teaching and taking care of her family, my sister, who was already in her forties, took on the challenge of commuting to Castries and pursuing her studies. She has since retired from teaching and with her degree in Counseling is looking forward to establishing a private practice. In light of such display of courage and determination, I began viewing my sister in heroic terms. Yet I shouldn't have expected any different from her. She may have been a difficult playmate, but you had to admire her fighting spirit, her killer instinct. The same fighting spirit that enabled her to dominate secondary school sports, setting the national long jump record at age fifteen, and that led her to represent her country in regional track and field meets and to becoming one of the most fearsome netball goal tenders you may ever come across.

The two middle boys didn't have the opportunity of a normal route to a secondary school education, because for them the transfer to the Plain View School came too late. But I suspect this wasn't the only complication. In the early days when my father was struggling to support a young family, he needed all the help he could get. So he insisted on the help of the older children, the boys especially, to make ends meet. Such that by the time my older brothers were fourteen or fifteen they were already driving my father's truck, helping to transport bananas, and were adept auto mechanics. My father also insisted that they learn tailoring, so they became part of his tailoring crew. In general, as the oldest boys at the time (my oldest brother had by then emigrated to St. Croix, USVI), they bore the bulk of the responsibility in my father's beekeeping, banana cultivation, and trucking operations. So while my father didn't go about deliberately or consciously selecting which of his children would pursue higher education, my older brothers' early concentration on practical matters and their early burden of bread-and-butter responsibilities would have left their minds less room to roam freely and playfully and may have placed them at a disadvantage with regard to educational pursuits. In comparison, although my younger brother and I were also part of the workforce that harvested the honey and bananas and carried out all the other family livelihood activities, the bulk of the responsibilities didn't fall on us; we never learned to sew or fix a vehicle or drive our father's truck. In fact, we were in our late teens but could barely drive. Our hands were on deck, yes, but our minds were free to roam. And on top of that, for us the Plain View School had come at the right time.

However, overcoming these disadvantages, after Plain View School, my brother, the third oldest son, three years my senior, decided to enroll at the Morne Technical College to pursue a two-year diploma program in joinery and woodwork. But no sooner had he graduated, he decided joinery and woodwork wasn't what he wanted to do with his life; he wanted to pursue higher education. So he enrolled at the SDA Academy, which, unlike the other secondary schools on the island, admitted students of all ages, and so was my brother able to attend secondary school at an age long past the cutoff age for secondary school students. By virtue of his technical college stint he was admitted in Form Two instead of Form One, and so found himself in the same form as my younger brother, five years his junior. With a mind already predisposed to practical things, school didn't come as easily to him as his younger siblings, and it didn't help that both boys were going to school and living in Castries on meager resources. But my brother preserved and secured a secondary school education. After graduation he taught for a while at the Vieux Fort Boy's Primary School and then joined me in the US, where I had just completed my first semester in college, to pursue his college education. Six months later, we were joined by our younger brother, who came to also pursue college education. So here the three of us were, deep down south in Baton Rouge, Louisiana, with no government scholarship, no financial backing of any kind, working almost fulltime, sweeping and mopping floors, throwing out garbage, serving as dishwashers in restaurants, flipping burgers at McDonalds, frying chicken at Popeyes Famous Chicken & Biscuits, on our way home from these jobs college students mooning us and shouting "Hey, niggers!" all this to put ourselves through college. Again, it was hardest on my older brother. He found it difficult to stay put at one place and concentrate on his studies, so it took him longer to complete his degree, but he persevered and earned a degree in medical technology. Following which he obtained employment in the blood bank department of a New York hospital's medical lab. To be fully qualified to work in the blood bank he had to take a licensing exam, preparation for which required his enrollment in a specialized program. My brother passed the exam at first try, and took great pride in the fact some of his colleagues who held master's degrees couldn't pass the exam. I was proud of him and it occurred to me my brother's bachelor's degree was as much of an achievement as his younger brothers' doctorate degrees. After passing the exam my brother was placed in charge of the blood bank.

My middle sister, the third child of the family and five years my senior, also has a heroic education tale to tell. As mentioned earlier, she was among the older children of the family who for one reason or the other missed out on the opportunity to acquire a secondary school education at the standard age and in customary fashion. Still, she refused to be denied higher education. So much so that in her early twenties, despite my parents' bare resources, she was able to convince them to send her to Trinidad to attend secondary school at the Seventh Day Adventist Caribbean Union College (CUC), well known for training Adventist pastors. I don't know why she didn't choose the less costly option of the SDA Academy. And for my struggling parents to have fallen for that, they must have indeed been suffering from guilty pangs about my sister, just there in the house, time passing her by, while her siblings were getting educated. Looking back, this must have been a case of overcompensation by my parents. Unsurprisingly, after a few years, guilt or no guilt, financial pressure forced my parents to transfer my sister to the SDA Academy, where she completed her secondary school education. Upon graduation she taught for a while at the SDA Academy, saved up, and about the time I was preparing to attend college in the U.S., she was able to (once again) persuade my parents to assist her with pursuing a degree at the Adventist West Indies College, renamed Northern Caribbean University, in Mandeville, Jamaica. It could not have been easy for my sister. Even with the help of my parents and some of her brothers and sisters, her finances allowed just a bare existence. Nonetheless, she completed her degree in 1982, about the same time I completed mine, following which she taught for a few years and emigrated to the U.S. in the late eighties to work and put herself through graduate school. She is now a licensed Counselor in the state of California.

The last of my parents' children to plod their way to college was the youngest child in the family, born a full eight years after my younger brother, then the last child of the family, when we thought my mother was too old to have babies. On the day of his birth, when my father came to pick us up at the Plain View School, he said with a broad smile, "Mama has made a little Prosper", which at the time I took to mean Prosper, the brother after me, was no longer the youngest member of the family; I had a little brother.

My youngest brother's entry into the world wasn't an easy one. My mother was thirty-eight when she had him, and he was born with a broken arm. Because of the broken arm, which would forever remain crooked, my brother never crawled. Apparently the arm was too weak to support his weight. So as a six-month-old baby, when his need for mobility became paramount, instead of crawling he made do with holding onto chairs, tables, walls, people, and whatever else he could grab that enabled him to move from one point to the other.

By the time my youngest brother entered his teens most of his siblings (his brothers especially) had gone overseas, so in my father's late middle age my youngest brother was the one accompanying him to the farm and on his trips to see his bees. After the death of my father, it was my youngest brother who took over his bee operation.

Graduating from secondary school, my brother taught for a while but by then pressure was mounting on him to follow in the footsteps of his older brothers and sisters and pursue higher education. Besides, he was my father's last hope of having a medical doctor in the family, because all of my father's other children pursuing university degrees had already chosen other disciplines. So in similar fashion as his older brothers and sisters, my brother joined the struggle in the U.S. of working and attending college. Initially, he did try to make good on my father's wish for a medical doctor. He majored and graduated with a degree in biochemistry, but then went no further in the medical or life science field. Instead, while working as a lab technician in California, he branched off to earn a degree in computer science and information systems, and so there went my father's last hope of a medical doctor.

But I'm being too hasty. Ever since my niece, my youngest sister's daughter, was a child she loved to hold and play with babies. So much so that she tested the tolerance of quite a few mothers of the Vieux Fort Seventh Day

Adventist Church on account of how much she bothered and played with their babies during church services. Unsurprisingly, growing up my niece has always wanted to be a pediatrician, taking care of children. Thankfully, with assistance from her parents and her aunts and uncles, she obtained her MD degree and is on her way to becoming a pediatrician. So my father finally got his wish (sort of), but sadly, thanks to the god-playing, reckless driver, he will never delight in it.

The two oldest boys in the family didn't get a secondary education, much less a college education, but they too have their tales to tell. Both started driving my father's vehicles at an early age, transporting passengers and bananas. At nineteen, my oldest brother immigrated to St. Croix and soon became a source of financial assistance to my parents, helping to support his younger siblings. In St. Croix, he worked as a heavy duty mechanic for Hess and operated a gas station, thus putting to good use the auto mechanic skills he learned while working with my father and when he used to escape from school. In the 1990s he returned to St. Lucia where he established a trucking and tire retail business, and lately he has also been trying his hand at farming.

Of all my siblings, my second oldest brother stayed home the longest, driving my father's truck, and lending a hand in his banana and bee keeping operations, while at the same time working as an auto mechanic and body repair man. In his late twenties or early thirties he and his wife emigrated to the U.S., not necessarily to pursue education, but in search of a better life. My brother is good at whatever the hands can do, be it auto mechanic/body man, welding, home repair and renovation.

Despite limited schooling, my two oldest brothers have accumulated as much or more wealth than any of their siblings. Their children are either college graduates or are college bound, proving that, notwithstanding my parents' commitment to education, there is more than one path to success, and higher education isn't everything.

As teenagers and young men, these two eldest brothers each in turn became notorious for their skill and daredevil approach to driving my father's vehicles. Being I was still a child when my oldest brother was making driving history, hearsay aside, I wasn't much of a witness to his exploits, but regarding my second oldest brother, no matter where he was going, be it to my father's farm or to the banana boxing plants to load up with bananas to transport to port, he was always accompanied by a bunch of Vieux Fort boys who came along for the lime and thrill and excitement of the drive. Up till today, these guys, now in their fifties and sixties, reminisce to me about those days of liming with my brother and of his driving feats in such glorious terms that I'm sometimes left with the impression that up to today this has remained the highlight and most fun-filled days of their lives. Of course, looking back I can well imagine what had brought fame to my brothers and entertainment to their friends must have brought financial distress to my father in the form of premature replacement of tires, shocks, brakes, and other vehicle parts.

SOME YEARS AGO, after reading *The Poisonwood Bible*, a novel by Barbara Kingsolver about an American missionary family's sojourn in the Belgian Congo, it suddenly occurred to me that I was of a family of heroes.

My parents' dedication to education, the hard work and discipline they instilled, and the life of integrity they preached and led had paid off handsomely.

Why Am I Writing About My Father?

WHY AM I WRITING ABOUT MY FATHER? What would my father think if he knew I was writing a book about him?

I'm not sure what my father would say. I suspect he would have been amused that I was going to the trouble of writing about him. But I don't think he would be surprised. By now my family have come to expect such and other unusual behavior from me. So the writing of this book was well within their expectations of me. After all, I'm the same person who at thirteen paid my parents a bedtime visit to present an historical and psychological theory of why each family member was behaving the way they did. I have forgotten what exactly I told my parents that night and why I had felt so compelled to share my theory with them. After all, it wasn't like I had a particularly good rapport with them. I'm also the same person who at eighteen handed a letter of resignation to my pastor, stating I was leaving the church because it no longer satisfied my needs and since

God resided in all of us we were all gods.

I'm writing about my father not because I was his favorite child, or the one closest to him, or the one who knew him best. In fact, given my childhood history of retarded, maladjusted and antisocial behavior (of which I will explain later), I don't think I could have been the one closest to any of my parents, nor could I have been their favorite child. I don't know who was my father's favorite child, but I suspect he was closest to my eldest brother. As the closest in terms of age, I think they understood and related to each other best. They were like business partners. My brother was in love with vehicles. As mentioned before, as a child he would *mawon lékòl* to hang around auto mechanic shops. My father too was very much involved with vehicles, though not necessarily out of love, but out of necessity, to earn a living. My eldest brother was the first of my three oldest brothers to work for my dad, driving first a van and then a passenger and banana truck. When at nineteen he emigrated to St. Croix during the 1970's St. Lucian migration wave to the US Virgin Islands, he provided my father with critical financial support from which the whole family benefited. And as my brother went into business — gas station, trucking, tire retail — my father became his chief business advisor, his confidant. For these reasons I suspect that among us my eldest brother was the one closest to my father. The one who understood him best and who knew the most about him. So probably he was the one best suited for writing a book like this.

To understand why I'm writing about my father, I may need to dwell first on why I write and then on what has predisposed me to being a writer.

Long before my writing life started, I used to have plenty of thoughts on many different subjects floating in my head, occupying space, bothering, suffocating me. Then I discovered that when I wrote them down I got a little respite that lasted at least until the next avalanche of thoughts. So it occurred to me the thoughts were begging for expression and were meant to be written down. I also discovered that when I sat down to write, a lot of issues inside me I never knew existed would come out. And oftentimes the material that would come to me to write was just a camouflage for what really was inside me, because what would actually come out once I began to write would look nothing like the original intent.

Why do I write? I suspect I write because there are things inside me that beg for expression. Things that will not leave me alone until I sit and write them down. I write for peace of mind. I write to get a clearer understanding of the subject of my writing. I write to find out what's inside me. My life is most complete, most gratifying, when I'm at work on a long writing project. Then, it doesn't matter what's happening on the outside. Writing completely absorbs me. It is one of the few activities when I'm at it, all the empty spaces of my mind are occupied. Therefore, it seems I also write for self-fulfillment.

When people realize that I write, they often comment, "You must really love writing." I'm always at a loss how to respond, because the comment isn't quite true. Often when I'm about to embark on a writing project, I procrastinate, trying as long as possible to avoid the painful process of sitting still for hours, day after day, with no clear idea of what exactly I want to say, and hence with little clue of what will actually come out. Plus there is always the chance that after all that pain and labor what comes out is garbage.

I suspect the essence of creation may have little to do with loving to create. After all, for some the process of creation is a lonely, painful and sometimes depressing undertaking. Just ask a woman in childbirth—the ultimate act of creation. The artiste at work may have nothing to do with love. Yes, relief after the work is created; drained, emptied, spent once the work is completed. Vindicated, maybe, when society has validated the effort. An artist creates not necessarily out of love, but out of necessity, out of compulsion. A woman gives birth not because she enjoys the birth process (yes, once the baby is born she often revels in her creation), for during the creation, in the middle of the pain, she, like Christ on the cross (a salvation creation), may have liked nothing better than to pass on the task to someone else. Toni Morrison, my favorite author, said she started writing novels because no one was writing the kind of novels she would have liked to read. So she wrote them herself. Inferring she may have been quite content to remain just a reader and leave all that writing business to someone else.

I'm not a natural writer. I have never loved writing. I'm not writing because I love to write. Reading, yes. I have always loved to read. So maybe I was drawn into writing because I love to read. But no, I do not write because I love to write.

Why then do I write about my father?

To date most of my writing has been about events, especially those that occurred during my childhood, that have left a strong and lasting impression upon me. My father's death, the suddenness and unexpectedness of it all, where one minute my father was alive and well and the next minute he was no longer there, would have to rank high among events that have left their imprint on me. So naturally my father's death was a candidate for my writing.

Perhaps I felt that if I could just bring myself to write about my father, then my mind would be more at peace; it would be as if I had breathed life into him, as if this would make him live forever, as if I had never lost him.

Art is a search for balance. When my father died something in me went out of balance, out of equilibrium, so writing about my father is probably my attempt at regaining some sort of balance, returning to equilibrium. When I started writing about my father, I wasn't sure whether I was going to be writing a book or just an essay. Nevertheless, I knew I would never regain my peace of mind if I didn't write about him.

Maybe if my father had died a natural death, whereby we would have had months of notice of his pending death, I would not be writing this book. But my father took his leave, or rather someone forced his exit, with no last lecture, no parting words of wisdom, no final blessings to help us continue the journey without him. No chance to let us know that he had made his peace with death, that death was OK by him, that he had lived a full and contented life. Suddenly and unceremoniously, someone, without any provocation whatsoever, had reduced him to a thrown away doll, as if his life was worth nothing, as if his life was a disposable paper napkin, as if his life had been about nothing. So maybe this is another reason I'm writing this book. To validate my father's life; to say, "Yes, there was a man called St. Brice Reynolds, father of nine children, who once walked upon this land and left a mark, left something behind for posterity."

Maybe I'm writing about my father to say the world was a better place with him in it. To say to the insurance adjuster who insinuated my father had long stopped being of value, and to the god-playing driver who by his action declared loudly and clearly that my father's life was worth no more than a doll that was no longer of use to a child, that my father was in fact of great value, had always been of great value, and, even though dead, continues to be of great value, because his wife, his children, his friends, his acquaintances, his brothers and sisters of his Adventist Faith continue being blessed by his memory.

Maybe I'm writing this book to ensure my father's memory lives on long after his children, his grandchildren and his great-grandchildren have joined him wherever the god-playing driver is keeping him hostage.

I also suspect I'm writing about my father to find out who he was, to get to know him better than I did while he was still alive. This may sound strange coming from a son whom he raised. But a look back may suggests that it is not so strange, that it is no exaggeration.

My mother's parents had eighteen children. Five died in childhood, leaving thirteen children, eleven girls and two boys, to grow into adulthood and old age. My mother and her siblings are a talkative bunch, anyone of them could effortlessly dominate a conversation. It is an amazing experience to have a few of my aunts together in the same room. At such times getting an audience with the president of the United States is likely to be an easier feat than getting a word in. I can just picture what it must have been like when they were all together under the same roof, and I wonder how my grandfather was able to cope.

My mother was by no means the most talkative of the sisters, yet it seemed next to work talking was her greatest passion. She could hold conversation with just about any-one. People came from afar to visit her. They knew time spent with her was time well spent. They got advice, history, news, herbal medicine, and sometimes my mother even talked them into doing a bit of work while they listened. Be-cause of my mother's predisposition to conversation, we learnt a great deal about her childhood days: her school days, her school fights, *ti boloms* (toddler-size supernatural beings devoted to do their master's biddings), coffin in roads, buried treasures lost and found, the life of her parents and those of her grandparents. And whenever my mother left something out, there was no shortage of aunts to help fill in the gaps.

Imagine this. My mother who hasn't been to England since she lived there over fifty years ago, still relates stories about her life in London as though she has just returned from there, and for the number of stories she has about Eng-land, you would never guess her stay there had been a mere two years.

Unlike my mother and her sisters, one couldn't get much out of my father and his siblings; they couldn't be described as talkative. On the contrary, growing up I was under the impression they were always deep into thought, deep into what was happening inside them. My father's sister, the one who cared for him after his parents were separated, was for-ever smoking a pipe. At such times she seemed so contented, so pacified, so at peace with herself that it often occurred to me that even if the entire world around her were destroyed, once she was left with her pipe, her satisfaction and contentment of life would diminish not one iota.

This non-talkativeness of my father's family made it difficult to get to know who they were, what their childhood was like, what were the personalities of their parents. It didn't help either that my father and his siblings were of an older generation than my mother and her siblings, and while most of my father's children grew up knowing both of their maternal grandparents, they didn't know their paternal grandparents because my father's parents were dead before his children were born. Thus my siblings and I grew up knowing much more about our mother's side of the family than our father's. So much so, when I'm thinking or talking about my family, it is usually my mother's lineage I'm referring to. That's why it was no overstatement when I said perhaps part of the reason I'm writing this book is to find out who my father was.

I suspect this not knowing as much about our father as we probably would have liked was compounded by his leaving for England during the great post-World War II West Indian migration wave. I was then still in my mother's womb and my eldest sibling, my oldest brother, was eight. When my father returned about five years later, I suspected he may have become a stranger to most of his children. Most of his children may have forgotten who he was. Because of this his children may not have related to him very well, at least not as well as they related to their mother. And it didn't help matters much that my father wasn't a man of small talk, wasn't a man given to talking much about himself, his experiences in England, the kind of conversation that would have broken the ice and begun the process of bonding with his children. So I can well imagine the typical misunderstandings and misinterpretation of words, actions, and silences that occur between parents and children when they are not properly bonded, arising between my father and his children. The result was that there may have been distance between my father and most of his children. Distance that may have outlasted his life. Of course, I may be making more out of the situation than is merited, because probably the norm in that era was that a father's role was to lay down the law and bring home the bacon, and didn't include sitting around chitchatting with children.

If there were any exceptions to the limited relationship that may have existed between my father and his children, it would have to be with his first two — my eldest brother and sister. These two may have been old enough to have already bonded strongly with him before he emigrated to have remembered him when he returned and therefore may not have seen him as a stranger, or an intruder, or a guest who needed to be tolerated.

My father left his children in search of a better life for them, but it seems that in the process his children had drifted away from him. They were there to greet him, yes, but they no longer remembered him. In his absence, some of that special, unspoken emotional connection that occurs naturally between parent and child might have been lost and maybe never fully regained.

I don't know. I'm not sure of any of this. I was the youngest of those my father and then my mother left behind when they went to England, so I'm probably the one worst suited for dwelling on these things. I'm dwelling on these matters because dwelling on the past has become a habit, a lifetime vice, a passion, even. Besides, maybe I got it all wrong. Maybe the situation of which I speak has nothing to do with my father's physical absence. Maybe despite his bountiful love for us, he had an inability to express his parental affection, or, when he tried, it came out the wrong way. Or perhaps what I'm saying here about my father relates only to me and not to the rest of his children.

A lack of closeness between my father and his children would have bothered him greatly for he was a man who cared deeply and sacrificed plenty for his family, a man who always preached to his children the value of sticking together and helping each other, a man who had such a loving and compassionate heart that people said he was too softhearted for his own good.

Once my younger brother and myself were under the bananas on my father's farm in Bellevue, Vieux Fort, having one of our famous discourses in which nothing is too trivial, or too momentous, or too sacred to wrap our minds around. I was about eight and my brother was about six. Somehow the conversation got around to my parents, and my brother said something to the effect that he loved his mother more than his father. Unknowing to us my father had overheard the conversation. A few weeks later—I don't remember the circumstances—my father reminded my brother of his statement. At the time, young as I was, my thought was: why should my father bother with what a six-year-old has to say? Why should he care that a child still wetting his bed (so to speak) loves his mother more than him? Now I can probably explain my father's feelings. Despite his best efforts—crafting kites, tops and carts for his children; bearing gifts of cashew nuts, mangoes, oranges, and plums from his farm, and candies, pastries, and Shirley biscuits from his trips to the capital; tolerating their fights over the scraps of his meals; beating them only sparingly — he may not have been as close to his children as he would have liked. If so I can well imagine his then youngest son's preference for his mother was like insult added to injury.

I have hinted that the reason why it is me and not another of my father's children who at this point has chosen to write about him has to do more than anything else with my fascination or addiction to the past, to history. It is fair to say this appetite for history also has something to do with why I write, and hence why I'm writing about my father.

Before my father went to England I didn't know him and he didn't know me, for I was still in my mother's womb. My mother left to join my father in England when I was at most eighteen months, severing the mother-child bond that was still in the making, a bond that would never be made whole again. I was too young to remember how I felt when my mother left. Still, based on what I have been able to catch, here and there (my mother wasn't comfortable talking about it), it must have been very bad. They say I was born sickly and was very attached to my mother. So attached that when she tried to wean me from breast feeding and switch me to the bottle at seven months old (two months older than when the other children had gotten on the bottle), I got very sick, forcing my mother to resume breast feeding. They say I was born prematurely, so I needed more care than most, and that was why I had been so attached, so dependent on my mother. Obviously, she had been more than my world. They say after my mother left I suffered from withdrawal symptoms, I didn't eat for days, I kept looking into every room for my mother, and I went up to women asking them if they were my mother. They say I lost so much weight that I looked just like a famine child. They say I used to shit on me standing up. The picture of me that comes to mind is one of a crack baby shivering from an addiction whose source he cannot fathom and so has no way of pacifying the addiction.

When my mother returned from England, I was about three years old, but I didn't accept her as my mother. After all, she was right there yet I would go up to women and ask, "Is you my mother?" To complicate matters further my mother returned with my ten-month old brother, who clung to her at every turn, crowding me out, denying me any chance of regaining my place, or of the mending of the severed bond.

I don't recollect rejecting my father when he returned from England. Maybe I saw him as a stranger, but never did I go around asking men if they were my father. Maybe because I never knew him it never felt like I had lost a father. On the contrary, it must have felt like someone had pleasantly surprised me with the gift of a father. With my mother the story was different. I must have known and felt I had lost a mother, because why should I be going around searching, asking for one? One only searches for that which one has lost. When my mother returned and I was told she was my mother, it must have felt like someone was playing a trick on me, telling me a woman who didn't look or feel like the mother I once knew was my mother (or maybe I had become programmed never again to be so attached, thus never again to be so hurt). So faced with this prank, I behaved the only way I could. I rejected her and instead went in search of my real mother.

Love is a two-way street. How does a mother who is already suffering pangs of guilt for leaving her children in the care of others (even if to prepare a better life for them, and even if it was in the care of her father and sisters), children for whom she has and continues to sacrifice, deal with the rejection of her three-year-old, the youngest of the lot she left behind? What did it do to her to see her own child walk up to women and asking, "Is you my mother?"

I don't know. For sure it would not help the situation. So the damage continued. I was afraid of my mother, I couldn't stand being in her presence, couldn't stand looking into her eyes. So much so, I felt like a stranger, no, a prisoner in my own home. Instead of endearing her, I saw her as an enemy, an enemy to fight, to keep at bay. I did everything to undermine her authority. I pitted my will against hers. I did everything in my tiny, three-year-old power to let her know I was certain she wasn't my mother, certain she couldn't be my mother, certain I didn't want her to be my mother.

The result of this travesty, tragedy, even, was antisocial and maladjusted behavior. *Tibway-la ka fou* (the boy is going mad); *Tibway-la dèkdèk* (the boy is retarded), were the common phrases people employed to describe me. I spent all my childhood and most of my teenage years with a cloud hanging over me: intense mental stress, oscillation between severe depression and wild, undecipherable behavior. As far back as my preschool days, I knew something was wrong with me and I knew whatever it was had to do with my mother, had to have started with her leaving for England. Right through secondary school, I spent the greater part of classroom time angsting over what was wrong with me, trying to decipher why I was acting the way I did, trying to solve the puzzle of my life: how old was I when my mother departed for England, and how old was I when she returned? Was she really my mother? My mind was constantly in the past, because somehow I knew there lay the answers to why I was the way I was, why I wasn't the person I was meant to be. Sometimes I was in the classroom, but instead of focusing on what the teacher is saying, I'm there imagining getting hit by a truck, yet suffering no injuries except that the blow to my head has shaken my brain and put right what was wrong with me. It was a period of unbelievable mental stress, it was too heavy a burden to carry for so long a time and from such an early age. It colored, suffocated my life.

The seriousness and realness of my childhood trauma was underscored in the metamorphosis I underwent at the age of twenty-five, in the Fall of 1982, two months after I started graduate school at Louisiana State University in Baton Rouge, Louisiana. Indeed, except for October 2, 1958, when birth was first given to me, this experience was undoubtedly one of the most traumatic and frightful experiences of my life. For in many ways I was reborn, my first life gave way to my second. What caused it? Why did it happen at this time? I don't know, except to speculate my childhood trauma had placed a kind of padlock or seizure on my mental, emotional, and physical development, and the metamorphosis of which I speak marked the beginning of the unlocking of that padlock.

The experience was a mass of sensations, all encompassing, all concurrent. During that period, my mind, body, and senses or feelings were in tumult. I became very timid and hypersensitive. The sudden timidity and shyness I felt were not unlike the behavior of a two-year-old clinging to his mother's dress on coming into contact with strangers. Every so often, spasms would shoot through my body, and my body would tremble as if I were experiencing the aftershocks of a terrible accident. It was as if someone concluded that during the first time around I wasn't born right. So the person arbitrarily placed me back in my mother's womb where I was safe and in want of nothing. Then suddenly, Fall of 1982, that same person rudely interrupted my haven, pushed me down the birth canal, and then without notice, instead of being enveloped in a sea of warmth and satiation, I found myself surrounded by bright nights, scary sights, strange sounds, and hunger. I felt like a turtle caught without its shell, a caterpillar caught in the process of changing into a butterfly, a snake caught in the middle of shedding its skin. Clearly, my second birth must have been almost or just as traumatic as my first.

These sensations were associated with a much scarier phenomenon. There was the gradual disappearance of the old me and the steady emergence of the new. During that time there were two persons in me. I developed a dual personality. I almost lost the sense of who I was. My mind was split between the past and the present. Sometimes I found it difficult to remember the past. The past became like a faint figment of my imagination. Other times I couldn't distinguish the past from the present. Still other times, I lived completely in the past. For a while there I thought I was going over the edge, I was going insane.

Many of the bodily functions which I had always taken for granted became unlearned. Suddenly, I was a baby again. I found myself having to relearn how to speak, how to walk, how to write, how to play soccer. Like my mind, my body became very uncoordinated, much like a one-year-old stumbling in the process of learning to walk, or a teenager going through puberty.

Stranger things were happening. My whole body was loosening up. My limbs began to operate much more independently of each other. I became keenly aware of my bodily sensations. My fingers acquired greater sensitivity. My mind became freer. Increasingly, I became better at self-expression. In the past I had had difficulty putting into words what I perfectly understood. So to do well on exams I had to not only understand class materials but memorize the sequence of words. In this my second life all that changed. Just understanding began to suffice.

I became more aware of my surroundings and became more sensitive to the feelings and emotions of others. I was traveling in a new world, but I had no map to give me direction. I had reached an emotional, mental and physical frontier. My mind felt like it had just been relieved of a life-threatening distress. My body felt like huge loads had been simultaneously lifted off my head, shoulders and limbs.

Most frightening of all these occurrences were my nightmares, which during that period occurred nightly. In my sleep I would be looking upon a pond in the middle of a lush meadow and then suddenly the tadpoles swimming in the pond would turn into menacing toads as large as breadfruits, and sometimes the toads would turn into rattle snakes poised to strike, and then into alligators with jaws wide open. Some other times one of the toads would swallow all the others and become as huge as a hippopotamus, with multiple toad heads. So horrifying were these nightmares that going to bed became an act of torture.

And what made this experience worse was that while it was going on I still had to meet the demands of graduate school; I still had to attend classes, study for exams, complete assignments; I still had to be mixing and socializing. All the while no one, not even my brothers, my roommates, knowing I was in the grip of the crisis of my life.

This whole born-again phenomenon occurred in cycles. The first cycle was the most dramatic. However, each subsequent cycle left my body, mind and feelings freer. The process was much like an earthquake and its aftershocks. Although the earthquake is the most dramatic and does the most damage, each subsequent aftershock adds to the total damage. Only in my case the earthquake and aftershocks that ushered me into my second life were for the better. Moreover, in my case, the aftershocks have continued to this day. But they have become almost imperceptible; the making of my second life is complete.

WHEN I LEFT HOME FOR THE US, my youngest brother was ten. Surprisingly, he was the one I missed most, the one who entered my dreams most frequently. I would dream of him, me making sure he was happy, contended, well-loved and wanting of nothing. Him enjoying the perfect childhood. My dreaming of him has continued up to today, though less frequently. So awhile back, I was forced to conclude that the dream wasn't about my brother at all, but all about me. After all, my brother was no longer a child but a grown man. This apparently was my mind's way of healing, undoing my damaged childhood, my damaged psyche. My childhood trauma had been so severe that my mind had to play tricks on me to repair the damage. With this understanding, I wrote the following poem, called *The Healing*.

I left you, oh so many years ago,
at the mimicking age; you aping my every word,
action and stance. And I, who from the time
you were born, had promised myself
you and I would be a family within a family,
cherished your attention like a guru his
favorite devotee.

I left you, oh so many years ago,
and crossed an ocean to seek education,
fame, and fortune. But little did I know
out of all the people I left behind
you were the one I would miss most,
you were the one who would never depart my memory.
You are locked in time, at the mimicking age,
in my memory, in my dreams. You, who are now
twenty-eight, six-feet, two-hundred pounds,
are locked in my memory at the age of ten, the age
you were when I departed for foreign soil.

I dream ever so often of the child I left
behind, him looking earnestly into my eyes
for direction, for approval, for self-definition.
I dream of showering him, who is locked
at ten years old in my dreams, with love,
protection, guidance. I dream of him having
a perfect childhood. A childhood where love abounds

and he is wanting of nothing. Though you
are no longer a child, this dream keeps occupying my sleep.

So this dream set me pondering.
Is it really about you who are locked in
my memory at the mimicking age, or is it about me
reliving my childhood the way I wished it had been,
healing the wounds of my seedling years.

BESIDES THIS BORN-AGAIN EXPERIENCE and the dreaming of my brother, how did I overcome this my childhood predicament, this sense of something being wrong with me? Of course, overcome may be too strong a word, for one can never fully overcome childhood trauma; no matter what healing takes place scars will remain. So a more useful question then is, how was I able to come to terms with this childhood disposition?

I have said before that from day one I hated school and it was the discovery of two of my greatest loves — books and soccer — at the Plain View School that changed my attitude toward school and made school bearable and sometimes even enjoyable. Well, books did something else as well. In them I discovered I wasn't alone, there were people who had suffered from worse predicaments than me, people who were blind, crippled, abused, neglected, and yet had been able to surmount their adversities to live extraordinary lives. Thus books, reading, was, I think, the first step of coming to grips with my abnormality.

Then came college education, which armed me with the analytical tools to examine my life, to decipher what was wrong with me. Education also led me to realize that no one is perfect, and even the most normal person suffers from inadequacies, that normality depended on who was asking the question; and also that my predicament and the childhood behavior that flowed out of it weren't my fault, the circumstances that led to it weren't of my doing and as a three-year-old I weren't responsible for most of my actions, I couldn't be held accountable for rejecting my mother.

Lastly, my writing. And so it would come as no surprise that my first major piece of creative writing, and to date my most lengthy piece, was an autobiography, written a few years after obtaining my Ph.D. Writing about myself forced me to come face to face with my childhood demons and in great detail because that was one of the demands of the writing. I was forced to relive my life and so gained greater clarity on what had transpired. The writing demanded I provide explanations for other people's motivations and behavior and so I gained a wider perspective on my life and that of family members, and the whole exercise allowed me to put things in better perspective. Writing did nothing less than enable me to gain self-knowledge and self-understanding.

My parents always placed great emphasis on education and left no stone unturned to ensure their children got their fair share of it, and I'm certain their main objective was economic, to ensure a better life for their children. Ironically, little did they know that from my perspective the best use I have made of education has been less about material things than about self-therapy, self-catharsis, self-healing. And, ironically, school, the thing I had taken such a dislike to, is the very thing that has saved me from myself.

It has been some time now since I have solved the riddle of my life. But the habit of digging into the past for answers, the habit of self-analysis, the habit of going internal for answers remains. And while I have been relieved of the burden of mental stress that used to cloud my existence, the habit of carrying the stress remains, so in its place a mental vacuum crept in. It's like a man who has been carrying a load on his back for many years and so has adopted a permanent stoop. One day the load is suddenly lifted, but the stoop doesn't suddenly disappear. He has developed muscles and fortitude to deal with the burden, so relieving him of it leaves him in discomfort, his body is expecting a load, so it is as if his body is begging for a replacement load.

Since the old mental burden was gone, my mind went in search of other mental burdens and so entered my writing. The mental effort and agitation associated with writing has now replaced the mental stress of previous years, and feeds into the old habit of self-analysis, of going internal, of delving into history. Solving the mysteries of my past, and the vaporization of the mental suffocation has made room for other engagements. Writing sits well with this abnormal predisposition of mine. It puts me back into my comfort zone.

It is not only that I want to write, I need to write. If I were to stop writing, then I would have to find another activity, another project to satisfy this craving for mental preoccupation, else my life would be unsettled, there would remain an unfulfilled yearning.

Still, it was one thing for me to have a need or compulsion to write, but an altogether different thing to accept the role of a writer and make it into this lifetime habit that has now led me to write about my father. Because when I started writing, I used to wonder, why me? What about me has led to this writing? What right do I have to force my writing, my thoughts, on the world? What is the source of my legitimacy? Is there something different or special about me?

These questions were particularly relevant because as I have indicated before I'm not a natural writer. Writing didn't come easily to me. In fact, without the modern technology of the computer and word processing software that allows automatic grammar and spell checks and effortless-cutting and pasting, I would not have been a writer.

I couldn't have been a natural writer because growing up I had an unusual speech and writing impediment. It was almost impossible for me to translate my thoughts into spoken or written words. I was always able to do well enough in school to move on to the next stage, but school work was a last minute, getaway game. I usually did class assignments, especially those that involved writing essays, at the last minute or not at all. Putting my thoughts on paper was like being in a nightmare in which I'm being chased by a monster, but something is holding me back, preventing me from running away. Nevertheless, as the monster stretches out his hand to catch me, my fear is so great I'm forced to concentrate all my energy, break the spell of immobility, and escape from the dragon in the nick of time.

When sitting exams, I would waste most of the exam time on the first few questions, trying to come up with the right words to capture what I wanted to express. It was so bad that the exam time would be almost over, yet half of the questions were still unanswered. At that point, under the panic of failure, I would abandon exactitude, grammar, spelling and punctuation marks, and in a frenzy of writing I would just barely complete the exam. So throughout secondary school and right into my Ph.D program, I answered most exam questions in the final minutes of exam time.

Because of the difficulty of giving expression to my thoughts, I was forced to come up with my own language. A language developed under extreme pressure, and thus one that had no time for grammar, punctuation marks, and proper diction. Now this worked fine with family and friends, people who had accepted this idiosyncrasy of mine as a form of retardation. At school it also worked somewhat with subjects other than English, but when English was the subject, this language of mine spelled doom. So this was why English was my most dreaded subject, and why writing didn't come naturally to me; and if it were not for the computer and my addiction to the past and my strong need for mental preoccupation, I would never have become a writer.

It was only after I had completed my master's and embarked on my Ph.D. that it occurred to me I was going to be writing books. How did I come to this realization? By then I had become aware that most things I read, I had either come across similar material or just by stretching my knowledge base a little I could have come up with similar analyses. In other words, reading was no longer the fresh, tantalizing, beguiling activity it once had been. This suggested to me it was time I started writing my own books. I didn't know then what kind of books I would write, whether fiction or non-fiction. All I knew was I was going to be writing books. This notion that I had to be an author was later reinforced by the dream in which someone asked: what would be my biggest regret if I were to die tonight? and to which I answered: there was no book in any bookstore or library with my name on it.

The notion I was destined to be a writer was further reinforced when, in late 1991, while browsing a newspaper stand, I came across a tourist magazine with an article on Derek Walcott, stating that Walcott had been mentioned twice in a row as possible nominations for the Nobel Prize and concluding it was inevitable he would eventually win it. Before this article, I was only vaguely aware of Walcott as a poet and playwright. I was unaware he was such a prominent writer. After reading the article, I hastened to the bookstore and picked up a copy of Walcott's *Omeros*. I was in for a treat. Here is Walcott talking about me, about the place of my birth and upbringing, about the way I feel about my people and my country. I read *Omeros* twice, and since then I have bought and read most of Walcott's plays and poems. In Walcott's work I found many gems. It was there for the first time I found out about the *charboniers,* the women coal carriers who, balancing hundredweight baskets of coal on their heads, were chiefly responsible for unloading and uploading coal onto ships at the Castries wharf during the era of steamboats, when coal was used as fuel. It was in Walcott's work also that I found out shabine means "red nigger." From just line of one of Walcott's poems, I was able to visualize the coal-carrying operations of the *charboniers,* which, in my novel, *Death by Fire*, allowed me to write a whole passage describing the *charboniers* in action. Later, when I was working on my second book, *The Struggle for Survival: an historical, political and socioeconomic perspective of St. Lucia*, I found a picture carried in the National Geographic Magazine and taken in the 1920s of the *charboniers* in operation. The picture matched almost exactly the image I had formed from Walcott's poem.

So you could well imagine how I felt, when, on the

evening of October 8, 1992, a few months after reading the article on Derek Walcott, straight out of work, I flicked on the television, and as if by magic, there was Derek Walcott being asked what winning the Nobel Prize meant to him? I jumped from the sofa and screamed, oblivious of my neighbors. Immediately after, I started calling close friends, spreading the news. But this was not enough, so in the morning I brought donuts to work and kept an impromptu breakfast party to celebrate with my American colleagues. But this still wasn't enough. So Saturday evening, I kept a house party to celebrate with friends. At the party, we watched a documentary on St. Lucia, and offered a toast to Derek Walcott and St. Lucia. I remained in a state of pride and excitement for quite awhile, so I wrote a tribute to our Nobel Laureates, which was published in the St. Lucia *Voice* newspaper.

A year after Derek Walcott won the Nobel Prize I received even further reinforcement on my destiny as a writer when I switched on my television and there a writer whom I was seeing and finding about for the first time was being interviewed. I asked myself, "Who is this thoughtful and regal woman?" She was Toni Morrison, an African American. Next day I hurried to the bookstore and bought one of her novels, *The Bluest Eye*. From the first sentence of that novel, I fell in love with Toni Morrison's work. She has written eleven novels and I have read every one of them three, four times, and still counting. Why this fascination with Toni Morrison? Well, there are two reasons. First, she has that uncanny ability to get to the essentials of an entity, the essentials without which the entity would no longer be what it is, and then she colors those essentials so they become in full view, in the process making the entity more of what it is. Second, Toni Morrison writes the way I think. Just imagine the thrill of reading an author who speaks the way you think! Discovering Toni Morrison was one of the best things that have happened to me in my adult life.

Later that same year, when Toni Morrison won the Nobel Prize in Literature, I started thinking what a coincidence that just a few months after discovering Toni Morrison she should win the Nobel Prize; but then I said, almost out loud: "Hold on, wasn't that the same thing I said when Derek Walcott won the prize? Coincidence my foot, someone is trying to tell me something!" And considering my dream about what would be my biggest regret if I died now, I said to myself that something must be I was meant to be a writer.

As with Toni Morrison's novels, I keep revisiting Walcott's work, and on each visit I am always amazed at the depth, breadth, and richness of his writings.

Nonetheless, even after such reinforcements and having two of my books published, I was still questioning my legitimacy as a writer. What right do I have to be imposing my writing on the world? Who appointed me a writer?

In confronting this issue of my legitimacy, it began to dawn upon me that many great writers, artists and creative thinkers are people who were born and raised on the fringes of society. They were outsiders. Derek Walcott talks about being a divided child, a *shabine*, a red nigger, a child of European and African ancestry. He also talks about growing up as a Methodist looking on Roman Catholic rituals and pageantry with a feeling of missing out. This dividedness made him different and so placed him at the edges of St. Lucian society. The writings of and interviews with V.S. Naipaul, the Caribbean's newest Nobel Laureate, clearly suggest he didn't fit in anywhere, he was the consummate outsider.

An examination of my life suggests I too have been an outsider all my life. My strange and abnormal relationship with my mother made me a stranger in my own home. And as a Seventh Day Adventist in a town and a country that was 90 percent Roman Catholic, my family and I were strangers in our own culture. At twenty I migrated to America, but as a black person and a foreigner I was a minority within a minority, so my outsider status was even more acute in the US than in St. Lucia. I returned to St. Lucia twenty years later. I'm no longer an Adventist (and even if I were, I wouldn't be much of a minority any longer because with over forty churches Adventism has gained a much larger share of the population), nevertheless, I have come back with an American way of seeing and doing things and a level of education that sets me apart from most of the population, so to some extent I'm a stranger in my own country, and it seems I'm destined to remain forever an outsider.

To show how much of a misfit I was in my own home, consider this. My mom is from Desruisseaux, a farming community in the southeast interior of the island. As children we accompanied her there on her visits to her mother's and sisters' homes. Years later I met a cousin in upstate New York, the son of one of the aunts we used to visit with our mom. He told me that all the time we used to visit them, he never knew I was a member of the family. He thought I was just a little friend of one of my older brothers. I couldn't stop laughing, because he crystallized my home predicament exactly. My deportment was so different and so out of step, that even my own cousin, never mind a stranger, had no choice but to conclude I wasn't part of my own family, that I didn't belong.

But what is it about this outsider status that sits well with writing and other intellectual pursuits? I suspect that while the outsider status can be painful and lonely, as an outsider one gets special vantage points, and one is forced to go internal, to search for answers to why one is different. It is this very outlook, this sense of imbalance, this sense something is missing, that becomes the raw material for art, for writing, for intellectualization. The writing of this memoir is a perfect example. The sudden and accidental death of my father destabilized my life, my entire world. In seeking a return to equilibrium and coming to terms with his untimely death, I was forced into introspection and so his life became the subject of this book. The habit of critical, honest, objective analysis one develops from analyzing oneself is in turn applied to society in general. This is one reason that has been put forward to explain why Jewish people, for instance, have contributed a disproportionate share of the world's creative thinkers.

Being an outsider in my own home placed distance between me and my family, distance that allowed me to look at my family as an entity separate from myself, and thereby a candidate for study, analysis, criticism, even. An idiosyncrasy that has made it possible for me to write about my father and my family. I have also been an outsider in the societies of which I have found myself part, so the same holds true for them.

Notwithstanding, I continue to feel uncomfortable calling myself a writer. So realizing that when Toni Morrison won the Nobel Prize she had written six novels, I said to myself, "If she can win the Nobel Prize with six books, surely that number of books should qualify me as a writer." So although in this memoir, for lack of a better word, I'm calling myself a writer, I'm being an imposter for plenty more work remains before I can honestly accept that title.

The preceding conversation explains why it was possible for me to write about my father. But it doesn't explain what prompted it. Again, what probably incited me to write about my father was that suddenly, without any sign, omen, premonition, or night-before dream, my father was taken away from me. So his death unsettled me, sent me into disequilibrium. It didn't help I didn't know him as well as a son should know his father. Writing about my father is probably my way of getting to know him better, and my way of accommodating myself to his death.

A Rendezvous With Death

THE MORNING OF MY FATHER'S DEATH, on my way to work, I had passed an accident on the St. Jude's Highway. I glanced at one of the cars involved in the accident, but seeing it had not suffered much damage, I concluded the accident wasn't serious and I didn't bother to stop. A friend at the scene of the accident waved at me, but thinking it was just a wave of acknowledgment I simply waved back and continued. Never did I realize the accident I thought wasn't serious had already claimed my father's life, the wave I considered a greeting was a death announcement, and the person doing the waving was one of the victims of the accident, the one whose car I thought wasn't too badly damaged.

Looking back, it seemed I had known all along the truth of the accident and the message contained in the wave, but apparently I wasn't ready for the truth, I wasn't ready for the reality of my father's death. I needed to buy myself some time. So I drove all of the thirty miles (a full hour's drive) to Castries only to be told my father had died from the very accident I had paid little attention to and had run away from.

So strong was my self-denial that even when the managing director interrupted my coffee brew to bring me news of the accident, I had refused to understand what he was trying to say. It was only after I called home and my sister said, "Daddy is dead, come home," that I could no longer deny the truth. I had run away from death, but now I had no choice but to go meet him. So as if watching someone in a slow-motion movie, I went to my car to begin my journey of reckoning.

As I drove out of the parkway of my workplace at Vide Bouteille, Castries, I made a decision. "Daddy is dead, nothing can bring him back, so I'm going to take my time to drive. The worse that could happen is for the family to lose another life." I followed my own counsel, I drove slowly and carefully, as if I were still learning to drive, as if I were going down that road for the very first time, as if I were going on a journey into the unknown. I suppose this was my excuse for taking as much time as possible to get home, my excuse for postponing the inevitable, the moment of truth.

Occupied with the death of my father, I expected the world to match how I felt inside: I expected Castries to be at a standstill; I expected rain and dark clouds; I expected bleak empty streets. But the sun shone brightly and there was no rain on the horizon and the city was buzzing along as it always did. The harbor with its verdant surrounding hills stood in its usual splendor. A couple of cruise ships berthed at Pointe Seraphine were boldly announcing the country's loss of sovereignty. Left of the harbor, the government high-rise buildings, St. Lucia's version of skyscrapers, built at the extinction of Conway, were still there ushering Castries into the 21st century.

I left Castries, its riotous produce market, its stench of human congestion, its offensive heat and humidity, its *mélé* of tourists and locals, its waterfront tourist vendors selling St. Lucian culture made in Guyana, and began the uphill climb along the recently built $70 million Tunnel Highway turned Millennium Highway, thereby avoiding the hairpin bends, though shorter route, that takes one through Morne Fortune, hill of fortune, the site of many battles between the French and the English. I don't know what fortunes Morne Fortune has brought to be so named, but on this drive I was feeling anything but fortunate, and preservation, not time, was my greatest concern.

Driving through the tunnels and descending into the broad expanse of the Cul-de-Sac Valley, to my right the picturesque Caribbean Sea and the Hess oil storage complex, straight ahead in the far distance, misty mountains, I was infected with the feeling that I'm about to enter a big country that always comes over me on passing this way.

The Cul-de-Sac Valley was once blanketed with bananas and before bananas sugarcane, but now large portions of it have been taken over by industry and cattle grazing. It is one of St. Lucia's three great agricultural valleys that served as the seedbed of the island's labor and political movements and the crucible of its democracy and nationhood. In 1907 a company of twenty-two policemen fired into a crowd of striking workers in this seemingly peaceful valley, leaving four dead and twenty-three wounded.

Taking my time, half my mind on the road, the other half

on death, I left the Cul-de-Sac Valley, drove through the village of Bexon, then the twin villages of L'Abbaye and Ravine Poisson, villages that were wiped out by the great 1938 landslide that claimed 92 lives.

My thoughts then left the scenery completely and went internal. I thought, how will my mother take my father's death? Was my father's death just the beginning? Did it mean we had lost favor with God, and had He stopped protecting us? What evils had my father been holding at bay that would now be unleashed upon us? Would it be field day, *bal fini, violon an sak*, from now on? Was this the time we would start paying for sins of the past?

I said to myself, "You see this, when you think everything is under control; when your life is going exactly as planned; when you begin thinking what and who you have become is due to you and you alone, that you are better than most, that the less fortunate are so because they have messed up, they have made wrong decisions; when the future looks like it can only get better; when your biggest worry is how much of a pay raise you will get this year, or whether to sell your house and move to a bigger one, or whether you should update or upgrade your car, or what choice of secondary schools your child's entrance exam grades will enable, or where best to spend your next vacation; something happens—your father dies, a routine visit to the doctor reveals cancer, without any warning your wife or girlfriend leaves you—that radically changes your life, changes your conception of yourself, yet there is nothing, absolutely nothing you can do about it."

Since my return from America, I had spent three years without working. Three years depleting my savings. Then just when I was making plans to return to the US, I was offered the position of senior economist at the Eastern Caribbean Telecommunications Authority, a job tailor-made for me. The job was in the same field as my work in the US and it allowed me to be in St. Lucia, the place at this juncture in my life I would rather be above anywhere else in the world. And as icing on the cake, being a regional appointment, the job involved traveling to the various islands of the Caribbean thereby providing me with a welcome opportunity to get to know the region better, one of my stated reasons for moving back to St. Lucia. And bam! only two weeks into the job, my father who since I had applied for the job asked me about it every time he saw me, even to the point of annoyance, is killed in an accident. What can I do to change that? Nothing. Absolutely nothing.

I climbed the Barre de L'Isle, a mountain range that runs lengthwise down the center of the island. The Barre de L'Isle or island ridge may as well have been named the badlands, for it was the excavation of this mountain to build the highway that eventually led to the catastrophic 1938 landslide.

Up in the Barre de L'Isle the road was clothed by forest and wedged between mountains that to the right rose into a patchwork of cultivation and to the left first dipped into the Cul-de-Sac River then rose to become Forestierre. The temperature dropped several degrees, giving the impression I had suddenly entered a temperate country.

Completing my ascent and then descent of the Barre de L'Isle, I entered the Mabouya Valley where my father lived after his parents were reunited and where the nephew who had tried to kill him now lives. The Mabouya Valley is another one of St. Lucia's great agricultural valleys. It too has played a pivotal role in the island's history and has had its fair share of agricultural labor protests, including the 1993 banana strike in which police shot dead two striking farmers, the aftermath of which led to a restructuring and liberalization of the banana industry. As I approached the second of three bridges in this region, to my right, a memorial built to honor the martyred farmers came into view. A plaque in the memorial reads:

IN MEMORY OF
Two Banana Farmers
Killed By Police On
Oct. 7th 1993 During
Protest Action For
Better Prices For Our
BANANAS

It was in this same valley, in 1957, in the middle of a sugar strike, that Mr. John Compton, renamed Sir John Compton, who afterwards would dominate the politics of the island for three decades, faced the barrel of the gun of the owner of the sugar factory when, as a labor union leader and district representative, he went there advocating workers' rights. In this same sugar strike, Mr. Compton probably saved the life of Mr. George Charles (then minister for social services who would, as chief minister, head the first government of the people and by the people) when he pushed the minister out of the way of a thrusting bayonet of one of the police officers deployed to squash the strike.

On both sides of the road snaking through the valley, banana fields stretched to the foot of the hills that to my left rose to become Aux Leon and Derniere Riviere. But caught in the throes of one of the worst droughts in forty years, the banana plants were dried up and shriveled, forcing one to ask what were the farmers fighting for?

My drive out of the valley took me uphill, then downhill into the smaller La Caye valley, then uphill again and downhill alongside the fishing village of Dennery. When I was growing up, Dennery was known as the witchcraft capital of St. Lucia (or maybe all the villages had such a reputation). My mother had a sister who made her home there. On visiting our aunt, out of fear someone might put witchcraft on us and turn us into nitwits, we the children made sure no one from Dennery patted our heads. My aunt's husband who was much older than her, died in his eighties. Shortly after his death my aunt took sick. She lost her appetite for food and drink. She had no detectable illness. She had simply lost her will to live. She died not long after her husband. Apparently, she couldn't, or refused to live in a world he was no longer part of. This to me was love in its most uncompromising form. I wondered once again how would my mother take my father's death? Will it be downhill for her from now on?

Dennery is also known as snake country. Both the boa constrictor and the deadly fer-de-lance can be found in its environs. There have been stories of farmers arriving at their destination with fer-de-lances curled up among the hands of the banana bunches they were carrying on their heads. The fer-de-lance, I was made to understand, is not native to St. Lucia. It was allegedly brought in by plantation owners to dissuade the African slaves from escaping into the hills. And apparently when the fer-de-lance got out of hand, the mongoose was brought in to keep them in check. The escaped slaves were called *neg marons*, runaway niggers, which came to mean savage, ignorant, unschooled; a connotation that no doubt was helped along by the plantation owners.

I thought of my father. The sadness of his death. In many ways he was in his golden years. For most of his life he had suffered from a bad leg. In his youth he had fallen off a bicycle and broken his leg. The break had not healed properly. His leg remained bent and it gave the appearance he was (and walked) crooked. Worse, though my father never complained he was in constant pain. So with his painful, crooked leg and walk my father kept bees, planted bananas, harvested bananas, made copra, loaded bananas onto his truck, transported bananas for the St. Lucia Banana Growers Association, transported people to Bellevue and Castries, stayed up all night sewing, preached on Saturdays, Sundays, Wednesdays and at crusades, yet the only way you would know he had a bad leg was from his crooked walk and his nightly massaging of the leg with a hot water bottle. It was only in 1997, five years before his death, through the initiative of my brother, the professor, and the financial contributions of his children that my father had an operation in the US that straightened his leg and provided him with some relief after more than half a century of pain and suffering. Fully recovered from the operation, my father's walk suddenly became youthful and he started his early morning walks and even some jogging.

And several years before this operation we, the children, helped our parents build a home on the outskirts of Vieux Fort, along the St. Jude's Highway, thus enabling them to leave their dilapidated home in the town and move to the suburbs. The house was built on a lot adjacent to my oldest sister's. She had built her home there a few years earlier, thus my sister's and parents' homes were side by side; it was like an extended family compound that operated as one yard and one household. My sister and my mother got along like two sisters. They shared the cooking duties of the two households and my sister took charge of tidying both houses. More importantly, my sister being a nurse meant that my aging parents had their own personal or in-house nurse. She accompanied them on doctor's visits, made sure they took their medication on time, and she regularly tested their blood pressure and sugar levels. The kindest, gentlest, and most selfless and conscientious soul you will ever find, my parents couldn't have asked for a better caregiver than my sister. I had no doubt that her caring of, and closeness to, my parents (my mother especially), both in terms of proximity and friendship, would have lengthened my father's life by quite a few years, had not the god-playing driver reduced him to a discarded paper doll.

Ironically, it was while on one of his early morning walks along the St. Jude's Highway that my father's life was snuffed. So the very operation that had brought him relief from pain, had brought him death just a short distance from the new home we had helped him build. So when we thought we had done our father a good deed, we had simply hastened his death. What kind of justice is that?

I could say with assurance that my father was in his golden years. The years where the only thing left for him to do was to enjoy the passing of the days. All his children were grown, were on their own, and could be considered successful. His days of stress, aggravation, and worrying about how he was going to feed, clothe, and educate nine children were ten, fifteen years behind him. His daily routine went like this: Up at six, have Bible study and prayer with his wife, go for his morning walk, have breakfast, take a morning nap, watch BBC, CNN, NTN and the Discovery Channel, watch cricket when there was cricket, talk with visiting friends, talk politics whenever the opportunity presented itself, sleep intermittently, watch the evening news and sometimes a night movie, go to bed at nine. A few times a month he visited his hives and three times a year he harvested his honey. He attended church on Saturdays and sometimes on Sunday and Wednesday nights. Once a month he went into town to pay utility bills. Occasionally he fixed such things as leaky faucets and through plenty of coaxing and nagging from my mother helped in some of the household chores.

So golden had my father's years become that my mother complained he was watching too much television, that he had too much time on his hands. In fact, when I was getting cable television for my father as his Father's Day gift, my mother wasn't pleased at all. She said he was already watching too much TV. Don't bother to tell her the man has worked hard all his life and he is well into his seventies so why can't he watch television as he pleases. She would tell you she herself has worked hard all her life, she also is in her seventies, yet she hasn't taken a rest. No use asking her whose fault is this? She finds work where most people would search with a toothbrush and find none.

My father's life had become so laid-back that his biggest aggravation was my mother's complaints about his television watching and that he slept on him all the time. How can one make sense of a man toiling in pain without complaint most of his life, only to lose it without cause just when he was beginning to enjoy some respite?

I climbed uphill away from Dennery. A few minutes later I bypassed the entrance to the newly constructed fifty-million-dollar jail the government built to house 500 prisoners. Months before completion I had paid the prison a visit. Already it looked like a college campus.

Soon I arrived at the farming and fishing community of Praslin, which, as an extension of Dennery, was well known for its snakes. Next came Mon Repos, a farming village and a bastion of cricket and St. Lucian culture. It is home to Dame Marie Selipha "Sessene" Descartes, regarded as St. Lucia's Queen of folk culture and one of the country's most celebrated cultural icons. All along my drive, the banana fields appeared to be in their final death throes. They seemed begging for someone to take them out of their misery. A far cry from the late 1980's, when banana fields spread out in verdant and vigorous splendor.

A few miles after Mon Repos, I arrived at the village and district of Micoud, home to St. Lucian cricket greats Marshall Francis and Darren Sammy, the latter being the first St. Lucian to play for the West Indies cricket team in any format of the game, and the only St. Lucian to captain the team. Micoud is known as John Compton country, for it was a bastion of the once John Compton-led United Workers Party and it was from this secure political base Sir John Compton ruled the nation and became one of the most successful and longest lasting political figures in West Indian history.

The drive out of Micoud took me across the Troumassee River, once the largest river in St. Lucia, navigable by small ocean crafts, but now thanks to the clearing of the forest to make way for bananas and other crops, the river has been reduced to a trickle. I wondered how many of the island's rivers will soon dry up for good, and how soon would the country have to import water for its survival?

Part of my mother's roots is in the Micoud area. Her maternal grandfather was the offspring of a Descartes (then owner of the Descartes estate) and his *dogla* (mix African-East Indian) maid.

I drove past the Desruisseaux gap, the winery at Canelles, the small fishing inlet of Savannes Bay, the Pierrot gap, and then suddenly the land flattened out and opened up and for the first time since leaving Castries I didn't feel engulfed by mountains and I could look into the distance without my view being blocked by one land mass or the other. A far cry from the many twists and turns and steep inclines and declines I had encountered along the way. This change of landscape was a sure sign that I was approaching Vieux Fort.

At the bend near Kitch Beach Cafe, under the flight path of aircrafts landing at Hewanorra International Airport, a sudden gust of salt-laden Atlantic breeze hit me in the face, providing another reminder that I was about to enter Vieux Fort. No matter how sick or tired I am from a Castries drive, this breeze, the taste of salt on my lips, always revives me, and I have always thought of it as Vieux Fort's way of welcoming me home. But today, rather than reassuring me, the breeze only awoke me to the reality of my father's death and that in a few minutes I would come face to face with the inevitable. The beautiful Atlantic waters at Pointe Sable Beach is another welcoming sight on approaching Vieux

Fort. So appetizing is the water that no matter the time of day or my disposition, on passing by I'm always tempted to take a dip. Yet today, despite the spray of ocean mist in my face, a sea bath was the furthest thing from my mind.

What was on my mind was how will I handle my father's death? When I reach home, how will I react? What will happen inside me when I see my father's body? People would have already started gathering at home, could I face them? Could I uphold myself? Will I break down into sobs? My brothers and sisters in the US will be coming down. How are they taking it? Is it harder for those away? Again I worried about my mother. What is it like to lose a husband of over fifty years?

The sound of my tires changed as the two-lane asphalt road ended and a four-lane concrete roadway built by the Americans during World War II began. The four-lane roadway gave the impression that one was about to enter a big metropolitan city. This isn't the only World War II legacy of the Americans. They transformed the entire Vieux Fort area into a military base. In the process they built a network of roads and runways, sewerage systems, water treatment plants and water reservoirs, a military hospital, now called St. Jude Hospital, and a dock for ocean-going vessels. To build Beanfield Airport, which was later extended by the Canadians and renamed Hewannora International Airport, the Americans changed the course of the Vieux Fort River to flow more westerly. At Moule-a-Chique peninsula, the southernmost tip of Vieux Fort and St. Lucia, they installed radar and other military facilities.

During the time of the Americans, Vieux Fort became an overcrowded boomtown of prostitutes, fun-seeking and

free-spending soldiers, and workers from all parts of the island and beyond who came to take advantage of the un-
precedented employment and high wage opportunities the
construction and maintenance of the military base offered.
The overnight population growth of the town caused serious
sanitary and health problems. And although the Americans
bequeathed Vieux Fort unparalleled infrastructure, histori-
ans have posited that their coming helped inculcate a lasting
habit of dependency; as if to say the town is still waiting for
an American second coming.

One of the enduring stories of the World War II American occupation of Vieux Fort, (later dramatized in a play by
Stanley French, a member of the 1950s St. Lucia Arts Guild
that set off a cultural renaissance in St. Lucia), concerned a
local man who was shot by an American soldier as he tried
to enter the base. Some say when the funeral procession arrived at the cemetery to bury the man, they found no body
in the coffin. Another of the enduring stories was that pros-
titution became so rampant in the town that venereal diseases reached epidemic proportions. So much so that the
Americans, themselves the original source of the diseases,
began bypassing Vieux Fort altogether and instead sought
their pleasures in the neighboring village of Laborie. Playing one-upmanship on them, the Vieux Fort prostitutes
changed their hair and dress styles and even their accents,
and presented themselves in Laborie as fresh, unspoilt ladies
ready to satisfy the Americans' every whim.

Before the Americans, Vieux Fort and its environs were
part of a sugar plantation. After the Americans the area re-
verted to a vast empty plain where grazing animals roamed
freely. This together with its rugged Moule-a-Chique penin-

sula (home to the world's second highest lighthouse), its southernmost location, its angry Atlantic shore, and its off-shore twin Maria Islets (a swim to which many a boy tested his manhood) has always made me think of the town as the last St. Lucian frontier. However, evidence of this frontier is rapidly disappearing. The center of town is pushing east-ward towards the Atlantic, and except for the area occupied by the airport, the town's suburbs have crawled across its surrounding plains.

I love Vieux Fort. I like the forever angry Atlantic Ocean on its eastern borders and the peaceful Caribbean Sea at its front to the west. I like the open, green pastures and the low-lying hills of La Tourney, Derriere Morne and Beause-jour that interrupt the plains. I like the unvanquished Moule-a-Chique, allowing ships safe passage and guarding the southern boundaries of the island. I like the mountains be-yond the low-lying hills that mark the end of the Vieux Fort plain and which rise to form Pierrot, Bellevue and Grace. I like the idea of animals grazing freely in open pastures, even the herds of cattle I often have to give way to for several minutes when they are crossing the road. The same cows that have written-off a vehicle or two and with which I have had several close encounters.

Early mornings, when I'm on my way to Vieux Fort from Augier where I reside and which is less than a mile from my parents' home, early enough to give me the sense the world was freshly created and just for me, after rounding the bend by the Marina, behind me the tips of Morne Gimie and the omnipresent Pitons, but straight ahead Moule-a-Chique kindly looking down upon me, greeting me good morning; to my right the Vieux Fort River, its waters blending with that of the Caribbean Sea; to my left Hewanorra International Airport, the tall green fields that encircle it, a few white cattle egrets on the green, marshy fields enjoying breakfast before the sun warms up; beyond the airport, beyond the Vieux Fort plain, the mountains still clothed in the early morning mist, reinforcing my sense of a freshly created world, I rejoice that I was finally able to say good bye to America and return home to stay.

But as I left the town behind me and swung right on to St. Jude's Highway, which would take me past the suburbs of La Tourney, La Ressource, and Cantonment then to my father's death, I wondered whether Vieux Fort will ever mean the same to me. For I had never envisioned a Vieux Fort without my father. My concept of the town has always included him in it.

From Vieux Fort my mind traveled to Guelph, Ontario, where I lived during the 1989-1991 period and where I was a visiting professor at the University of Guelph. There I became friends with a Western Samoa couple and their two daughters, one five and the other seven years old. While visiting me one evening I showed them my family album, and, with no warning whatsoever, the younger of the girls pointed at a photo of my dad and asked, "Why is he so sad?"

I was a bit taken aback because the little girl asked the question with no prejudice, no malice, no preconception of my father. In fact, at the time she pointed at the photo, she didn't even know the man was my father, and I couldn't recall ever having said anything that might have given them the impression my father was a sad man. So I had to take the child's observation seriously. It occurred to me there may be truth and clarity in her innocence. She must have seen something that we adults, preoccupied with the problem of living, may have missed. Her question, though embarrassing—for it is not a pleasant thing for a stranger to point out one's father is a sad man—forced me to look more closely at the photo of my dad, forced me to see more concretely what maybe I had sensed but had never given voice to. There was no denying the little girl was right; the photo did suggest there was a sadness in my dad.

Strangely, nearing home soon to meet death, I wondered: could my father have been described as sad? If so, over what part of his life was he in a state of sadness? If so, why the sadness? Was it because of circumstances arising from his life? Regrets maybe that his life hadn't turned out as he had planned and hoped, that he hadn't achieved what he had set out to accomplish? Regrets maybe about the paths taken and the paths not taken; decisions made and decisions left unmade? Dissatisfaction maybe with his family life; disappointment with how his children had turned out? Loneliness and yearning maybe for his parents, his aunts and uncles, his brothers and sisters, all of whom he had outlived? Had the burden of feeding, clothing, and educating nine children while administering to his Adventist flock left so little time for self, so little time for self-indulgence, so little time for feeding the wellspring of self-renewal that periodically washes the sadness and pain of the world away and leaves one feeling the world was freshly created, and just for one? Did having to work too hard and too deep into midlife to keep his family afloat break his spirit? Assuming the photo wasn't playing a trick on the little girl, did this sadness creep in at the time in his life when he was no longer young but not yet old, the time when he began feeling his strength, his energy ebbing? The age when it began to dawn upon him that the future had arrived, he had become what he would ever be, and what he wasn't he would never be? That age when dreams and visions meet reality and reality wins hands down? The age when the mind can no longer trick the ego that beyond the bend lays a brighter future?

Or did my father's sadness, if the photo was telling the truth, have less to do with his life and more to do with the state of the world at large? To what extent were the tribulations and injustices (famines, earthquakes, wars, neglected and hungry children) of the world weighing down upon my father? Was he embracing too much of the pain and suffering of the world over which he had little control?

I don't know. It may well be that my father's face had nothing to do with what he felt inside. Some people have faces that seem in a state of perpetual anger but when you speak to them you are surprised to find out they are as pleasant as people come. On the other hand, there are some people who are always smiling but who are more vicious than most people you will ever meet.

Seated in my car and soon to meet death, I didn't know. All I could say was that the photo seemed to suggest a sadness in my dad. Yet I could also say that by the time my father entered his seventies, when for no reason the god-playing driver turned him into uselessness, he was enjoying his golden years. All his needs were well taken care of, he had no children on his account, and, according to the autopsy, he was in good health: no cancer, no stroke, no high blood pressure, no diabetes. He was also without pain, because, thanks to his children, the one pain he had, the result of his broken leg, had been taken care of five years before his death. Therefore, I can say with assurance there was nothing else my father needed to do in life but enjoy it and watch his grandchildren grow.

I PULLED INTO MY PARENTS' DRIVEWAY. A small crowd had already gathered. I reluctantly left the sanctuary of my car and went inside. My mother was still at the hospital with my dad; only my youngest sister was at home. The people there expressed their sympathies; I barely heard them but mechanically mouthed, "Thank you." I said to myself, "We will need to start serving these people drinks." So I looked in the refrigerator to check on the state of affairs. There wasn't much in the way of being hospitable. Yet I did nothing. I was numb, not feeling, barely seeing. I just walked around mindlessly. I could find no comfortable resting place in the house. I felt like I was at somebody else's home, a timid guest unsure of his welcome. As if it wasn't my father who was dead. Strangely, this was the way I felt throughout the funeral service, the burial, the wake, and for months after the funeral. Like an imposter, a hypocrite; like this death had little to do with me. I accepted people's hugs, their sympathy, their condolences with the feeling that what was happening wasn't happening to me at all. It didn't feel real. Nothing felt real.

My sister hugged me, and it was only after the hug I realized how much I had needed to be hugged. A little later she came to my rescue a second time when she told me we needed to get some drinks to serve the people. That I could understand. Action. Numb, unfeeling, feet-dragging action. This broke the spell. I was forced into motion, a motion that continued almost non-stop right up to the day after my father was buried. I went out to buy the drinks and the action saved me, because I realized that once I kept busy, kept active, kept moving, things would go easier.

It was in bed at nights and when I woke up early mornings with the realization my father was no longer in this world, that I suffered most and was forced to contemplate how could this have happened?

The unfolding tragedy of my father's death opened my eyes to other things. I hadn't realized people may come to a friend's funeral not just to provide comfort to the family but also to receive comfort. I hadn't realized that in some cases they needed more comforting than those whom they have come to comfort. For unlike the family of the deceased whose loss is tangible, definable, and therefore can be dealt with more directly, the loss to non-family members wasn't as definable, wasn't as tangible and was therefore more difficult to deal with. Another thing I came to realize months after my father's death was that when someone dies, especially someone close, people are reminded of their own past loss, so when they grieve for the newly dead, they are also grieving for their own loved ones, so in coming to the funeral to give comfort they gain comfort.

Before my father's death none of that had ever occurred to me. When it came to death I was naive. Attending funerals had never been high on my priority list. I hadn't realized how comforting it was to see familiar faces, to be embraced and hugged. How weak, vulnerable and helpless the death of someone close rendered one. And I hadn't realized how much comfort the singing that accompanied the funeral and burial services brought. Now that I know, I have a much greater respect for death.

By The Sweat Of Thy Brow

MY EARLIEST MEMORY is of my mother's return from England. I was three years old. As if from another world, she stepped off a horse-drawn cart, dressed in a white flowing dress, white gloves and white, wide-brimmed hat. I'm not sure whether this image, this memory, is simply a figment of my imagination or if I made it up as the years went by. I have never squared it with my mother's own version. It seems I didn't want this, my first memory, altered in any way for it has been with me ever since I know myself.

My second memory is of my mother baking bread in the early morning with my younger brother, the one born in England, still barely able to walk hanging on to her dress.

Although my father returned from England two or three years after my mother, I do not have such a clear memory of him on the day of his return. Maybe he arrived in the night while I was asleep. Nonetheless, unlike the homecoming of my mother, my father's arrival was anticipated weeks in advance. Among the older children who had a memory of him (or maybe it was my mother's younger sisters), the story was that my father was slow to anger, he didn't beat often, but when he beat, he did so with a rage. Thus I was probably waiting with great expectation but with some trepidation for the father I did not know, had never laid eyes on, who didn't get vexed easily but when he did, you had better watch out.

I may not have had a clear memory of my father's return, but I remember that after his arrival the house changed. My earliest memories of him are forever linked to foot-long scissors; giant pressing irons weighing upwards of twelve pounds and heated by coal fire; an abundance of thin, cardboard-like garment patterns; spools upon spools of thread; trunks loaded with cloth; flat, triangular white chalk; cloth trimmings all over the house; sewing machines crowding the living room. The tools of the trade.

Shortly after his return from England, my father quickly became known as one of the best tailors on the island, and one of the few tailors in the Vieux Fort area who could make three-piece suits. But this came at a price. With his bad leg, a damaged eye, and the constant harassment of eight children (the last child had not yet arrived), he sewed day and night, altering his sleep pattern for life, such that long after he stopped sewing and up to his death, no matter how much sleep he had, once inactive he would *sleep on him* anytime, anyplace, on any occasion. Rest assured that at home when my father wasn't sewing, or building hives, or preparing a sermon, or under the truck fixing something or the other, he was somewhere *sleeping on him*. He slept on the rostrum, in the middle of the Saturday church service, with such regularity it had ceased to be an embarrassment for us. In fact, once my father was up there and not preaching he grabbed some sleep. It was as if the many years of sleepless nights spent sewing had forever impressed upon him that sleep was such a scarce resource that whenever the opportunity presented itself he had to hoard it. He slept as if knowing tomorrow or tonight will bring sleep starvation.

I pitied my mother in those years that my father's sewing machine chewed away the night, and chalk and cloth dust suffocated the house. My mother's dream of a home or her image of how a home should be was forever thwarted. For years she quarreled about not having nice living room furniture, a proper dining room, a living room where furniture didn't have to compete with sewing machines, ironing boards, and trunks of cloth, a house and furniture free of chalk and cloth dust.

For his part my father behaved as if he never heard my mom's complaints, as if a home crowded with the tools and consequences of his trade was the most natural thing on earth, as if he couldn't envision any other kind of home. My mom got some respite, and her home began approaching what one should look like, only after my father's eyes had deteriorated to the extent that tailoring was no longer possible or feasible. But by then my mother was well into middle age.

In England my father picked up tailoring secrets so quickly and he had such a knack for sewing that he said he would have been rich if he had stayed in England. The Jews for whom he worked thought so too. They were so impressed with his progress and dedication, that they told him before long West Indians like him would be taking over England. My father had forgone the opportunity to be rich to be with his family. I have often wondered whether he couldn't have had both by bringing his family to England. I have never discussed that with him, but from my experience living in America I suspect he didn't want to raise his children as second-class citizens.

Interestingly, my father's tailoring had an impact on the the social fabric of his country. For I was told that back then to get married one had to have a three-piece suit, so since only the well-to-do or at least those of decent means could afford one, marriage was beyond the reach of many. And I'll bet ladies of the day were using ownership of a suit as an indication of a man's fitness for marriage and as a sign of his manliness.

My father was a tailor by profession and training, but to me he was most at home, most himself, most in his element when he was engaged in his outdoor occupations, be it farming or beekeeping. My father would be at home *sleeping on him,* but as soon as we boarded the truck and headed to the farm, a good five miles from town, he would suddenly become upbeat, alive and alert. With cutlass in hand, a blade of grass between his lips that he used as a whistle, my father would lead the way on our mile-long downhill trek from the road to our farm. Once in the country he was never in a hurry, his walk always leisurely. He stopped to greet and chat with the country folks we met along the way. Jokes aplenty, humor the likes of which we never heard around the house. You could sense he shared a great affinity with the rural folks.

My father loved the land, the bananas planted in it from which he derived a living, the trees and plants rooted in it from which he derived food, the animals that grazed on it, the birds that fed on the fruits of the trees rooted in it, the creatures that crawled on or bored into it. He was rooted in the land. There was a huge *mango palwi* tree standing in the middle of the farm. I always associated that mango tree with my father. To me, my father belonged to the land as much as that tree belonged to it. The river that empties into the Caribbean Sea near Vieux Fort passes through my father's farm, though at a more youthful stage. This river caused us plenty of grief, because raging or not we had to cross it to get our precious banana cargo to the road. Every time I come across a river it reminds me of this river, which brings back memories of my father, his children and the land that he loved.

Watching my father walk on his farm I got the impression that he knew by name every banana plant, every flowering tree, every blade of grass, and every hummingbird that fed on the fruits of his land, and before he left for home he had to say hello, pay homage to, or at the very least, acknowledge every single one of them individually.

On such visits to the farm, be it to harvest bananas or to gather dry coconuts for making copra or to collect our weekly supply of fruits and ground provisions, we the children were always in a hurry to return home to go play football or cricket or to watch a match. But to our great consternation, not so our father. It seemed to us that he did his utmost to delay as long as possible his taking leave of the farm.

Memories of my father, my growing up, and my family life are invariably linked with ceaseless work. For between my father's tailoring, my family's farming and beekeeping activities, and my mother's industriousness, our home, our house, was like a factory. A factory that was open six days a week, twenty-four hours a day, and in which my parents and us children were the factory workers. So in my family there was no time for folly. It was work, work, and more work.

Starting when I was seven years old, and my younger brother was five, twice a month, every month, my family got up at four in the morning, packed supplies and headed to the farm, where we spent all day, right into the early hours of the evening, cutting, assembling, packing, and carrying bananas on our heads, across a river (sometimes raging), uphill, downhill, uphill, downhill (sometimes muddy and slippery), along narrow walk paths and onto the road, the bananas making grooves in our heads, our feet saying they cannot take another step, our necks screaming they can carry not even one more feather. Yet we returned for another load, and another, and another, until every bunch of bananas was next to the road. And there we waited, sometimes past midnight, for the truck that would take the bananas to port, we the younger children so deep in sleep that we accidentally wet the dry banana straws that had become our mattress. But make no mistake. No matter how far beyond midnight we got home, the following morning we rose with the sun, school beckoning. On that there was no compromise. The only compromise, if you could call it that, was the day we had taken off to go on our banana odyssey. Bananas were our existence and school was our mantra.

But not according to my youngest sister who never took too kindly to this banana carrying odyssey. On banana days, waking her from bed was more difficult than uprooting a fruit-laden *mango palwi* tree. Sometimes when everyone had already boarded the van or the truck that would take us to the farm, my sister would be nowhere in sight, only to be found snuggled in bed, despite many earlier attempts to wake her up. It took nothing less than a serious beating from my father when his patience had finally run out to convince my sister that there was no escape from the family's banana carrying ordeal. That morning, the morning of the beating, we didn't feel sorry for her, because since we were already up we wanted to get on with it so we could return home as early as possible. But now, looking back, I must conclude she was the only sane one among us. Because to leave your warm, cozy bed, and step into the chilly predawn, and while you were still half asleep, board a transport that will take you deep into the chilly, dew or rain-drenched interior of the island, then to carry bananas on your small head, all day, each load, each trip to the road causing your neck to be as stiff as a stale loaf of bread, and to arrive at your home past midnight was madness indeed. In a different time, in a different country, my parents would have been accused, prosecuted and convicted of child labor.

My eldest sister was the only one who escaped our banana carrying odyssey, for by the time my father started cultivating bananas she was already in secondary school, and once in secondary school my father didn't allow us to skip school for the sake of bananas. However, we couldn't complain nor harbor any misgivings about our eldest sister. For if there were one person we didn't mind missing the banana harvest, it was our eldest sister. She was more than a big sister to us. She shielded us as much as possible from the rod of our parents. If she caught one of us in some wrongdoing, even if she threatened to tell my parents, we could rest assured she would never carry out her threat. Her quiet disposition, her soft, gentle, sensitive heart could not bear to see us, her younger brothers and sisters, getting hurt, suffering. Besides, she more than made up for missing the harvest. Without complaint she made all the beds, cleaned the house, swept the yard, washed the family's clothes and did the cooking. She was ever willing to sacrifice, to do without, for us to have some of the things we needed. She rarely asked for things for herself. She rarely complained, but was always there to console and encourage us. We couldn't have asked for a better big sister.

Carrying bananas was by no means our only torment. On Sundays and during school vacations, if we weren't carrying bananas, we dug holes, planted bananas, weeded bananas, fertilized bananas. And in between cultivating, harvesting and carrying bananas, we climbed coconut trees, picked the dry nuts, gathered them throughout the farm, peeled off the husks with cutlasses and pickaxes, broke them into halves, drained out the water, stocked them in washed-out fertilizer sacks, carried the filled sacks along the same route and on the same heads that carried the bananas, loaded them onto the truck, and when we got home we put them to dry ontop the galvanize roof of the house, and when they were dried we spent many afternoons after school separating the shell from the copra (the dried nut) and then ramming the copra into washed-out sugar sacs for transporting to the soap and coconut oil factory in the southwestern town of Soufriere.

And in between bananas and coconuts, three times a year we harvested honey. We stood next to the hives, our father intermittently smoking the bees, selecting the honey-filled frames and passing them on to us. We hung the frames in wooden boxes, bees, in spite of the smoke, stinging us every which way. We then carried away box after box of honey-filled frames on the same heads that carried the bananas, the fertilizer, the coconuts, the weekly collection of fruits and ground provisions, with bees climbing up under our veil stinging our eyebrows, our noses, our lips. When all the honey was assembled, we stayed up the better part of the night squeezing the honey from the comb, bees we thought long dead stinging our hands at will. We then strained the honey and filled several drums with honey for the market. The following day we went to school (and from this there was no escape because school was our mantra) with faces that looked as if heavyweight boxers had used them as punching bags.

On top of all that, my mother was always having us carry dung from the pasture, seaweed from the beach, and dirt from construction sites to build soil on top of rocks in the yard so she could cultivate her vegetable and herb garden. And as if that wasn't enough, we were constantly making bricks, first to extend the house, then to build a storage room, shower and septic toilet that replaced the outhouse, and then for the new house we would build someday but which never got built. Also, once a week, every week, we had to collect wood under the bush surrounding the dock which we carried on our heads back to the yard to fuel a stone-and-mortar oven in which my mother baked every Friday in preparation for the Sabbath. And to beat it all, the family factory was extended to include the church (proof that my father made little distinction between church and family), and as such we provided the bulk of the labor for making bricks to build the church and for loading and offloading my father's truck with sand for making the bricks. It was like we were the children of Israel under forced labor making straw bricks to build Egypt.

Town children weren't supposed to work so hard. But we worked harder than any family I knew, harder than most people in our town, harder than most farm people, even. This is why when I was growing up I was baffled that Vieux Fortians considered us rich. True, when my father returned from England he opened a tailor shop, and was quickly known as one of the best tailors on the island. True, my father was among the first few people in town to own a van or any vehicle for that matter, and when the van ran out he bought a truck that served to transport both bananas and people, and then he bought a car. True, we had a telephone and refrigerator before most of our neighbors, so it was to our home people came to make phone calls and to buy ice and to refrigerate their fish and meats. Our house was bigger than most houses in the neighborhood and, because of the farm, if not meat, we had an abundance of ground provisions, bananas, plantain, breadfruit, and all manner of fruits. But I always used to wonder that if we were so rich, why were we working so hard? I thought being rich meant a life of leisure.

The volume of work was bad enough, but what made matters worse was that the hard work wasn't balanced off with play. My parents, my mother especially, didn't allow us to go out on the playing field. According to them, the town was populated with the ungodly, people of the world, people who were in bacchanal, so if we went to play with the children of these ungodly people, they would corrupt us, turn us rotten, turn us into vagabonds. Yet we couldn't play ball in the yard, because the ball kept hitting against the house, breaking windows, disturbing my mother's naps. Thus before we could pick up bat and ball, we heard the never-changing shout, "Stop playing ball there and go get a book to read." So we became creative. On the hill above the yard we cleared the bushes and excavated dirt and rocks to create a cricket pitch. That worked for a while, but before long we couldn't play there either, the ball was entering my mother's garden, we were trampling her garden retrieving balls. So we did the only thing we could do. We turned into thieves. When my parents weren't home, or when we went to collect wood for the oven, we sneaked away to the playing field; and when my mother was taking her nap or when she was busy in the kitchen, we played hush, hush, hush in the backyard. The dreaded words, "Go pick up a book to read," or worse, "Come here, I will beat you, I'm tired of telling you don't go out on the field and play," always threatened. My buttocks and back still remember the beatings with hoses, buck end of belts and tamarind whips that I have received for going out on the field. So back then I would gladly have traded the so-called riches that Vieux Fortians said we had for a bit of the freedom I saw many of the town's other youths enjoying. Freedom to go to the beach anytime, freedom to roam the surrounding bushes in the area, freedom to play ball to my heart's content. Thanks to this legacy of my parents, working has become so ingrained in me that I cannot spend a day lying around doing nothing without feeling guilty that I'm wasting my life away.

To this day my mother who is now well into her eighties

still runs her house as if it were a factory, and in the process presents a lesson in multitasking. The rising sun catches her in her vegetable garden. In between her gardening tasks she prepares meals, processes and bottles honey, makes tamarind balls and gooseberry jams for sale and fruit juices for home consumption, she grinds turmeric and cinnamon sticks for spices, rearranges furniture, and holds court with visiting friends and family. Five in the afternoon would find my mother still on her feet. Yet she doesn't have to; she could just as easily take it easy. But if you were to tell her that, she would tell you she has never seen work kill anyone.

Now my family's industriousness and farming activities, and my father's love of the land have become fond memories. And it saddens me that the land my parents must have sacrificed so much to acquire and which helped sustain, educate and shape us is now taken over by strangers or is in a state of abandonment. Most of my father's children are scattered across America, and the few of us living in St. Lucia are too preoccupied with our own activities to bother carrying on his legacy. In Desruisseaux, where my mother and her siblings are heirs to an abundance of farm and forest land, this phenomenon has been carried out on an even grander scale. There is a spring on the land that never dries up. But again, many of my mother's siblings and their children and grandchildren are scattered across England and America, so the land has returned to strangers and to the wild. These thoughts used to occupy me for years. Then in 1991, I read *Omeros*, Derek Walcott's book-length, epic poem, and for the first time I realized that verse lends itself to some of my thoughts. It inspired me to write my first poem, *The*

Land is Crying, which gives voice to my thoughts and feelings about the abandonment of our forefathers' legacy.

The land is crying, the grandparents,
once devoted stewards of the land,
have joined the spirit world.
The parents, shaky limbs, weary
souls, precariously holding on.
The children have all left,
some in search of knowledge,
others in search of illusive treasures,
some others in search of excitement
and pleasure, each their own way,
the legacy of slavery has manifested.
Master living in grand style,
magnificent and opulent is his dwelling,
surrounded by the forefathers of the children,
they at his every bidding, toiling sweats
of pain on the plantation,
suckling the children of the master,
master bathes in luxury and style.
So a value has been passed on down through
the ages. To work hard is to be a slave,
tilling the soil is nigger work, conspicuous
consumption, lavished clothing, continuous
excitement and pleasure are things of the master.
Who wants to be a slave?
Slave no one wants to be, master
all want to be. So the children have departed
from the land in search of becoming masters.
* The grandparents told the parents:*

"go get a trade, slavery is no more,
tiller of the soil thou shall not be.
Better yet, cross the ocean,
go to the land of the masters
of your slave ancestors, learn the ways
of the masters, everything foreign is superior,
the greater the distance you travel,
the closer to the masters thou become."
The parents said to the children: "Go
get an education, or forevermore shall
thou slave on the banana plantation."
Damnation. Damnation.
The children are scattered,
the land is moaning in sorrow.
Parcels have been abandoned,
to the wild they have returned;
parcels, strangers have taken over.
Overwhelmed with loneliness,
the land is weeping, its bosom is empty,
its arms are wide open,
waiting for its children to come home,
waiting to reconnect with its seed.
Known treasures have the children
left, for treasures unknown.
Some are now sweating blood on foreign
soil, some are cleaning houses for the descendants
 of the masters of their forefathers,
just like their forefathers for their masters.
Meanwhile the wisdom and bounty
of the land are flowing to strangers and to the wild.
The river flowing through

the land has heard the cry and pain of the land.
The river is laughing noisily at the land,
while it continues to carry the land,
bit by bit, day by day, into the sea.
The trees tremble as they listen to the
sorrow of the land. The birds and the crickets
try with sweet melody to console the land
in its moment of grief.
The children have heard the
sorrow and longing of the land;
they have felt the ache
in their hearts and the hole that remains,
which once the land filled.
The land and the children, each the other needs
but can the children overcome
six generations of slave legacy?
Oh how wonderful it used to be,
the parents and the children, together,
tilling the land of their forefathers.
Together they stewarded the land and reaped its bounties.
Together they were, the land, the parents
and the children. Will they ever come
together again? The parents are
becoming the past, they are soon
to join the spirit world like the
grandparents before them, and the great-
grandparents before the grandparents.
The children are now the present,
and their children the future.
Time is running out for the meeting
of the parents, the children, and the land.

The children need to hear once more the stories
that the great-grandparents passed on
to the grandparents and the grandparents
to the parents. Now the parents need to
pass on these stories to the children,
so in time the children can pass on
the stories to their children and their children
their children.

Will the great relay of life maintain?

My Father Was A Man Of God

MY FATHER WAS A MAN OF GOD, and my family was more religious than any family I knew. For as long as I knew myself, my father had been the elder of the Vieux Fort Seventh Day Adventist Church. But he wasn't just the elder of the church, he was the bedrock of the church. No. He wasn't just the bedrock of the church. He was the church. He preached the Sabbath sermon, he preached the Sunday night service, and when there were no takers to lead the Wednesday night prayer meetings, he did that too. He contributed the most tithes and offerings, and when there was a crusade he provided the transportation, he provided the preaching, and his family provided the bulk of the singing. When the church decided to leave the house-turned-church that they were renting and build their own house of worship, my father's truck transported all the building materials, and his children, his family, provided the largest portion of the manual labor.

My father's life was so intertwined with the Church and its services that I learned more about him while he was on the pulpit than at any other time.

It was there that I learnt about his fight with the cigarette demon. My father said in his youth he had a way with women, so much so that even after he gave his heart to God, plenty of women used to trouble him. It didn't help that his tailor shop in the middle of town made him a natural magnet. Still, he had no problems resisting them, he was leading a new life, he was baptized, he was reborn in Christ. But what proved a stumbling block to serving his God was cigarettes. No matter how often he tried and how many times he quitted, he would always go back to smoking. My father was in deep agony. Cigarettes were robbing him of the Kingdom Christ had gone ahead to prepare for him, robbing him of a seat beside his Messiah. When my father could take it no longer, he went into the bush with a packet of cigarettes, smoked every single one, and then for three days he fasted and prayed, battling the cigarette demon.

Listening to my father on the pulpit relating this story, I would pictured Christ in the wilderness, weak and hungry from forty days of fasting and praying, besieged by the devil with one temptation after another. My father said that after he emerged from the bush no cigarette ever entered his mouth again, and he never once felt the urge to smoke. Like Christ he had finally been able to tell the cigarette demon, *Get thee behind me, Satan.*

I reckoned the reason my father lost the urge to smoke was that after enduring this kind of punishment—three days of fasting and praying under the bush—for just a little smoke, his mind and body reasoned that it wasn't worth it, so they banished the very idea of smoking from his thoughts. But it would take somebody like me, who doesn't walk with God, to think that way. To my father, it was God who had given him the strength to overcome the devil.

From the pulpit, my father said that when he bought a truck for the first time to transport people, the carpenter who was putting the hood on the truck pulled him aside and said, "Mr. Sedwan, listen to me well. You should look for a good *gadè* for that truck, you know. If not, is your time you wasting. Not even one passenger you will be able to pick up, for all the other trucks have their *gadès*."

At this point my father would tell the congregation how, after his conversation with the carpenter, he fell on his knees and prayed. He told God he was putting all his trust in him. He asked God to protect him and his family from the evils of the world, keep him in good health, and give him the strength and courage to continue serving him, and safeguard his livelihood so that he can continue to feed, clothe and educate his children.

Then my father's voice would rise in triumph, "Brothers and sisters, to this day God has not let me down. To this day my truck has not left Vieux Fort without a full load. To this day my family has not lacked food and clothing. Church, it pays to put your trust in God."

In response the church would come alive, "Amen, Brother Reynolds, Amen." With the help of God their hero, their leader, their role model had beaten the devil. Praise the Lord, they too shall overcome.

This wasn't the only instance where my father had benefited from putting God first. In his twenties he converted to Adventism after attending a crusade held by Pastor Sebro, a pioneer in St. Lucia Adventism. Soon after my father gave his heart to Christ, several times a week he would ride his bicycle all of the six miles from Vieux Fort to Desruisseaux to preach at a crusade. Unknown to him my mother was a regular visitor at that crusade. But it was in Vieux Fort, not Desruisseaux and not at the crusade, that my father first caught the eye of my mother, and one of the first things he said to her when he came chatting was, "Do you know who I am?"

My mother said, "Of course, I know who you are. You are the one preaching at Desruisseaux."

And as the saying goes, the rest is history. My father had forsaken Catholicism, his known world, and sought the kingdom of God and like a hero had gone into the unknown world to preach the gospel and at the age of twenty-six a nineteen-year-old bride had been added unto him.

Essentially my father's style of preaching was to take a story or stories, sometimes a bible story or one of his own stories, elaborate on it, dramatize it, embellish it, make it his own, and then draw from it lessons for better living and for serving God. To me, in my father's stories, he would take on, no, become the main character of the story. In the parable of the Prodigal Son, my dad was the long-suffering father pitying his wayward, wretched son, overjoyed that he had returned home, forgiving him, welcoming him with wide open arms, and chastising his other son for his selfishness and unwillingness to forgive his brother.

In "David facing Goliath," it was my father, one of a few Adventists in the town of Vieux Fort, facing the giant, the unbelievers, the blasphemers, the people of the world, the Roman Catholic priest, with just a slingshot, with just a bible, and with the help of the almighty God emerging triumphantly.

In the story of Job, it was my father, that in a test of wills, a test of steadfast righteousness, whom God allows the devil to rob of all his wealth, murder his children and cover him with sores from head to foot, reducing him to sitting naked in ashes. Yet despite all this he held steadfast, consoling himself with, "*the Lord giveth and the Lord taketh away. Naked came I out of my mother's womb and naked shall I return, blessed be the name of the Lord.*" It was my father who, after seeing how low he had fallen, his wife said to him, "*Dost thou still retain thine integrity? curse God, and die.*" But instead he rebuked his wife, telling her she spoke as a foolish woman.

My father's sermons, or his stories, if you will, always ended in triumph, and this one was no exception. Job's reward for never forsaking God when no one could have blamed him if he had, was the stuff of magic and miracles. He received twice as much wealth as before, he fathered as many and more beautiful children and he was blessed with such a long life that he saw four generations of his grandchildren. Once more, the lesson was that it paid to put your faith in God. Without fail, you will be rewarded beyond your expectations. In the end the wicked are always cursed and punished and the righteous blessed and rewarded.

This was the stuff I was brought up on. This was the stuff that shaped, colored, and gave my life form. Growing up, I believed wholeheartedly that the good are blessed and rewarded and the wicked are cursed and punished. But now, in midlife, I don't believe that anymore. It seems to me the world belongs to the aggressive, the greedy, the driven, those who are prepared to have their way no matter who gets hurt, and what is destroyed in the process. The good, the meek, the considerate, are forever running for cover. My father's godliness, his peaceful and loving heart, his commiseration with the downtrodden couldn't save him from the reckless twenty-four-year- old who took his life. So what do I believe? I believe that who lives, who dies, who gets wealthy, who remains poor, has little to do with good or evil and everything to do with effort, ruthlessness, habit conducive to the attainment of the goal, and the price one is willing and able to pay to achieve it.

Like many protestant denominations, the Adventist Church was very aggressive in trying to win souls. In St. Lucia, faced with a historical legacy of a population that was over 90 percent Roman Catholic, the most Roman Catholic of the English-speaking Caribbean, they had little choice if they were to make any headway. As the leader of the church and by far its best and most powerful preacher, my father was at the forefront of this crusade for souls. But the town of Vieux Fort was a tough nut to crack. Eight-week-long crusades would produce less than a handful of souls, and within a year more than half of these few hard-won souls would again be lost to the world. It appeared that in Vieux Fort the Adventists had as much luck winning souls as Lot had in finding righteous people in Sodom and Gomorrah. So faced with such odds, the church sought greener pastures in rural hamlets with names like Augier, Piaye, Gertrine and Pierrot.

When there was a crusade, the church boarded my father's truck on Sunday and Wednesday evenings and on Saturday mornings and headed for the interior. The grown-ups went to win souls, the older children for excitement and meeting the opposite sex, the younger children for the ride and thrill of seeing a different place. Sometimes the church held the crusades in tents and sometimes in dancehalls-turned-churches. When the kerosene lamps came on, and the singing penetrated the banana and coconut fields and entered homes, villagers seeking entertainment and sometimes God emerged from under the banana foliage, in ones and twos, and in groups. On a weeknight the crusade was their only source of entertainment.

One night of these crusades stands out in my memory. It was held in Piaye, a small rural community situated between the southeast villages of Laborie and Choiseul, about seven miles west of Vieux Fort. At this crusade, for three consecutive weeks my father had been proclaiming that whoever would come forward and prove that Saturday wasn't the Sabbath day, or that any day of the week could do just as well as Saturday, he, St. Brice Reynolds, would give that person a prize of a thousand dollars.

Finally, on this Sunday night of that crusade, a "Mission" (Baptist) pastor stood and took up my father's challenge. Now, it wasn't that my father had money to give away. It was just that he was so confident of the Saturday Sabbath that he couldn't envision defeat. Besides, for Adventists a lot rode on their Saturday Sabbath. This was the most important feature separating them from the other Protestant denominations. If not for the Saturday Sabbath, there would be no Seventh Day Adventist Church.

The "Mission" pastor came up, Bible in hand, confident he would leave the dancehall-turned-church with a thousand dollars.

My father went up first. He brought the pastor's attention to Exodus 20:8 -11. *Remember the Sabbath day to keep it holy* . . .

The pastor turned his bible to Matthew 12:1-13, where he showed that Christ healed people on the Sabbath day and allowed his disciples to pick and eat corn on the Sabbath, suggesting that the coming of Christ meant that the observance of the Sabbath as a day in which one's own doings weren't allowed was abolished. The pastor further explained that more generally the coming of Christ rendered the Old Testament redundant or obsolete, because most of the Old Testament activities were temporary substitutes for the coming of the Messiah.

My father countered with the argument that in Matthew 12:1-13, what Christ was trying to point out wasn't that the observance of the Sabbath as a day of rest and abstinence from one's worldly activities was done away with, but that it was all right to do good on the Sabbath, especially such things as caring for the sick and feeding the hungry that can't wait till the Sabbath is over.

Then he gave the pastor a Bible lecture. "If you read the Old Testament carefully, you will discover that it speaks of two types of laws given to the Jews. One set of laws, the ceremonial laws, which included such things as the offering of sacrifices, were practices pointing to the coming of Christ, so when Christ came such practices were no longer necessary. However, the testimonial laws, which include the Ten Commandments and therefore the Sabbath observance, weren't abolished with the coming of Christ. In fact, the life of Christ was exemplary of the upkeep of these laws." My father then directed the pastor's attention to Matthew 5:17-18. *Think not that I am come to destroy the law, or the prophets: I am not come to destroy but to fulfill.* And in triumph, his voice rising as the spirit of God came over him, my father turned to Hebrews 4:9-10. *There remaineth a rest therefore to the people of God. For he that is entered into his rest, he also has ceased from his own works, as God did from his.* And speaking more to the audience than to the pastor, my father explained that in the Hebrew language rest is translated to mean Sabbath.

By then the pastor had lost considerable steam. Besides, he was alone. My father's flock and the yet-to-be-converted people of Piaye surrounded him. But the pastor wasn't quite finished. A lot more than the thousand dollars was riding on that debate. Just a few months before he himself had held a tent crusade in Piaye, but the Adventists were undoing some of his work. Several of his recent converts were among the spectators. He couldn't afford to shame himself and lose this debate. The battle for souls had begun in earnest. He argued that the important thing is to worship on some day, which day was of no consequence. Besides, how do we know which day was the first or last day of creation? The naming of days is an artifact of man.

My father had heard this argument before and he was prepared. He told the pastor that according to the Bible, Christ rose from the dead on the first day of the week, and the whole world celebrates this first day as Easter Sunday. So since he has accepted Sunday as the first day of the week, by acknowledging that Christ rose from the grave on Easter Sunday, he can't go back and say that Saturday is not the seventh day of the week. Besides, argued my father, worshipping on Sunday has its roots in the pagan practice of worshipping the sun, and it was Constantine who decreed the change of the Sabbath from Saturday to Sunday.

The pastor mumbled some lame response, but by then it was clear to the audience that my father had won the battle. The pastor walked out. His last words were, "We will just have to wait and see who goes to heaven and who doesn't."

That night as the Church members rode home on my father's bus, they were high on the spirit. They kept telling my father, "Ahh, Brother Reynolds, you well catch him tonight, you well catch him." Never were they more proud of their elder, their hero, than the night he had won one for the Lord.

As for me, to this day the only way I can put my father's life in proper perspective, or the best I can picture him, is to place him in the company of such biblical heroes as Noah, Abraham, Moses, Job, and Paul of Damascus.

WE WERE SEVENTH DAY ADVENTIST and the time between sunset Friday and sunset Saturday belonged strictly to the Lord. For it is written: *Remember the Sabbath day, to keep it holy. Six days shall thou labor, and do all thy works: But the seventh day is the Sabbath of the Lord thy God: In it thou shall not do any work, thou, nor thy son, nor thy daughter, . . .* My family took this seriously, for it was the keeping of the Saturday Sabbath, more than anything else, that separated the Seventh Day Adventist from the rest of the world.

On Saturday mornings when we walked to church it seemed to me that the whole world was at a standstill, as if everything and everyone was in a state of meditation. The sun was rising more slowly, the wind was more calm, the animals in the pasture moved more leisurely, the town more settled and quiet. But this perception of mine had all to do with my inner state of mind and nothing with the level of activity in the town. After all, Saturday was the busiest shopping day of the week. While we were in church, the market where the farm came to town was bursting at its seams with produce and people. And the stores were overflowing with people from all the towns, villages and farms of the southern half of the island. Since most shops, except the rum shops, which never went to church, closed on Sundays, it was only on Sundays that the town truly quieted down. But to me and the other Seventh Day Adventists on the island, Saturday was the day that man, cities and nature stood still.

Now, all this church business was fine when I was still a child, but as I entered my mid-teens church burdened, suffocated my life. Church on Saturday morning: eight-thirty to twelve; Saturday afternoon Young People's Meeting: four to sunset; Sunday night service: six-thirty to eight-thirty; Wednesday night prayer meetings: seven to nine; and then there were the crusades and fasting and prayer revival meetings. Tired from a Sunday on my father's farm, many of these Sunday night services served as my bedtime lullabies.

But there was more. Next to the Sabbath, the second pillar, the other Bible passage that set Seventh Day Adventists apart from the rest of the world, was Deuteronomy, Chapter 14. Any land-dwelling creatures whose hoofs weren't parted and which didn't chew the cud were forbidden to be eaten. So were water dwelling creatures that didn't have both fins and scales. So we couldn't eat lobster, shrimp, crab, shark, *shadon* or sea eggs; we definitely couldn't eat pork chops, bacon, sausage, *souse,* or any other pork products; and we couldn't eat blood pudding or *bouden.*

Smoking and alcohol of any kind, in any quantity, were

forbidden and a cause for disfellowship. Still not satisfied, Adventists extended their list beyond the Bible. Coke, coffee, tea and other caffeine-containing products were forbidden. But this wasn't all. The adventist interpreted the biblical command of *do not sit among the ungodly* to we couldn't go to the movies, couldn't go to dances, couldn't participate in carnival, definitely couldn't jump behind the band, and couldn't attend the Roman Catholic First Communion masses and fetes, an activity more than 90 percent of the population engaged in because more than 90 percent of the population was Roman Catholic. In fact, we couldn't enjoy any of the island's cultural activities. For the culture of the island was synonymous with the world, with worldly "pleasures" and "abominations." Folk music, calypso, reggae, cadence, were worldly and corrupting and therefore beyond reach, beyond enjoyment. And we didn't celebrate Christmas. For according to the Adventist, there is no way Christ could have been born on December 25th. Because, the argument goes, how could a man and a woman about to give birth walk all the way from Nazareth to Bethlehem in the midst of winter, an eighty mile journey that must have taken anywhere from four to seven days? Now, you would think if the Adventist really wanted to pick a fight, a more serious objection would have been: how could a woman be with child without having had sex or some form of insemination or fertilized egg implantation? Now, if you could accept that, the question of winter seemed a mighty small problem to overcome. Never mind. Every Christmas time my father devoted a whole Sabbath sermon proving why Christ couldn't have been born on Christmas Day, thereby depriving me and my siblings of our Christmas celebration. True, on

Christmas Day my mother cooked special dishes: curried goat and dumplings; and she baked the finest of fruit cakes, so we ate better and more lavishly than at any other time of the year. But that was the extent of it. No matinees, no children parties, no bazaars. Essentially, I was denied my culture. At fifteen I still couldn't differentiate between reggae, cadence and calypso. I was awed at my so-called "worldly" friends having no problems deciphering which was which. So I am not exaggerating when I say that my Seventh Day Adventist status had rendered me a stranger in my own culture.

I couldn't escape my Adventist status. No. I couldn't. Being an Adventist in a town and country that was more than 90 percent Catholic and being at the forefront of the Adventist Church, my family was indeed a minority. We were marked. Our name changed. When we walked the streets, little children shouted, "*Semdays, One Week*."

I couldn't deviate one inch. I couldn't sneak to the movies, I couldn't go to a dance, I couldn't even yawn in public, because the townspeople, never mind the fact that they placed no limits on their own enjoyment, their own pleasures, were quick to chastise me with, "Not you all that say you all *Semdays*, and you here dancing like this; and you at the movies; and you playing ball on Saturday?" Forget about trying to get a girlfriend. If we were seen chatting up a girl, they would say, "You all *Semdays* eh you all want woman."

My oldest brother was the only one in the family who seems to have escaped the vise grip of the Adventist Church, for I don't remember him ever going to church or adhering to the practices of the religion. In fact, to me, he was just as "wayward" as any of the other young men growing up in Vieux Fort. Before he left for St. Croix at nineteen, he was my mother's biggest source of aggravation and the target of most of her quarrelling and nagging. When he left I was under the impression that the whole family rejoiced. We thought the house would finally have some peace, my mother would stop her nagging, and we the children would be spared my brother's surveillance and punishments. Of course, my mother never stopped her nagging. Her attention simply shifted to her husband and the rest of her children.

As I mentioned earlier, my brother was a perfect example of "do what I say and not what I do." He made a habit of skipping school, but would spank any of us who did the same. In fact, anytime he found us in a place where we shouldn't be, he would either spank us or carry a report to our parents. As a pre-teen, I was very much tickled that my brother got even angrier than my dad when a boy started befriending my oldest sister. He became my father's watch-dog, carrying reports on my sister anytime he found her with the boy. So in keeping us on the straight and narrow path, my parents got plenty of help from a very unlikely quarter—my oldest brother. It was only years later, after my brother got married and settled down, that, to what must have been my parents' great joy, he returned to the Adventist fold.

For me and the Adventist Church, things came to a head when I turned eighteen. By then I had already graduated from secondary school and was working as a laboratory assistant at the St. Lucia Water Authority. Around that time, as part of a journey in search of self, I started practicing yoga and was reading cosmic science literature, which led me to question the notion of God as presented to me by the church. I became convinced that we were all gods. God existed in all life forms. With such thinking I came to realize that the Adventist Church no longer suited my needs. Besides, I was no longer willing to remain distant from my own culture, and I was no longer willing to have someone dictate to me that I couldn't go to movies and dances, I couldn't play football on Saturdays, and I couldn't drink a beer. Furthermore, I was a bona fide *Dread*. I wasn't smoking marijuana, at least not yet, but I had bought into most of the Rastafarian philosophy, especially the part about living natural and my African-ness. I dressed it, I talked it, I walked it.

So at seventeen going on to eighteen, I braved the wrath of my father and formally resigned from the Church with a letter addressed to the pastor. Upon receiving the news, my father, furious, waited for me at the front doorstep, the same place he had waited several years before after I had repeatedly disobeyed him and gone on the field to play soccer and he had given me the worst beating of my life, a beating with the buckle end of his belt. This time things were slightly different. This time I was no longer a boy. I was now a man earning my keep and was quite prepared to live on my own, if need be. Moreover, I was a *Dread*, a radical, to all intents and purposes a Rastafarian. I came when my father called, but I refused to sit, because I knew that with the issue at hand my father was likely to fly into one of his rare and sudden rages. I wanted to make sure that I could get away in time if the talk so resulted. At the age of seventeen going on to eighteen, I wasn't accepting any kind of beating from my father, or anyone else for that matter. The days of the rod had long passed, I reckoned.

"Sit down," my father commanded, but I refused the offer. Instead, I just stood there, staring him down. I was prepared for any eventuality. Furious, my father shouted, "Get out."

I walked out.

I wasn't sure whether my father meant leave his presence or leave the house, so that night I slept in the truck. In the morning, I came home to find out exactly what my father had meant. He ignored me, so I concluded that he must have meant leave his presence, not the house. So I stayed home and didn't pack up and leave.

Despite my formal resignation, the church still took the pleasure of casting votes to disfellowship me from their membership, as if I hadn't already broken free on my own accord. I guess, this was one pleasure they would not be denied.

Though I was branded a backslider and became even more of a stranger in my own home, I had won the war. And from then on I did as I pleased: went to movies, went to dance halls, drank my Heineken and played soccer when and where I wanted, Sabbath or no Sabbath.

But my break from the church didn't do me much good when it came to the town's social circles. At dances, none of the girls would dance with me or even touch me. I don't know what it was. Maybe there was a light surrounding me that blinded them, burnt them when I got too close. Or maybe my presence spoiled their fun, reminding them of restraints and inhibitions they would rather banish from their minds. I was marked when I was in the church and continued to be marked long after I had left the church. So where and when the constraints of my parents failed, and I got a chance to break away, to free up myself, the town my parents tried so much to shield me from, came to their aid. My parents and their religion had insulated me from my culture, but now my culture was insulating itself from me.

Notwithstanding, my life has gone full circle, and gives credence to: "*Spare the rod and spoil the child;*" "*Train up a child in the way he should go: and when he is old, he will not depart from it.*" For in middle age, I drink sparingly, I don't smoke nor indulge in drugs, I stay away from pork and as a rule I don't eat red meat. In fact, coffee is one of my few vices. I exercise regularly, and generally I'm very conscious of my health. And though I don't keep the Sabbath, I try to abide by "*Do to others as you would have them do to you*", or "*love thy neighbour as thyself.*" Come to think of it, all my siblings, whether or not they are practicing Adventists, follow temperate and healthy lifestyles. Clearly, another legacy of my parents.

Unbashful Death

THE THING I HATE MOST ABOUT DEATH is the finality, the infinity, the no-return, the no-second chance of it all. I fear the closing of doors, the closing of avenues, the dwindling of possibilities. I hate the notion that taking one path means the exclusion or elimination of all others. Yet death is the ultimate restriction, the ultimate exclusion, the closing of all doors, the clogging of all paths. At no other time was I more occupied with dying than in my mid-thirties. I walked, slept and dreamed death. So occupied was I with death, that I wrote this poem.

As a child,
when immortality was within my grasp,
Death was missing on my list of rendezvous.
I thought becoming an adult was the defeat of
dependence, restrictions and punishments.

Now I know different, but then
I welcomed the aging process
like a princess her long departed prince.
Now, at the age of 35,
as Death slowly creeps,
it has become my bedside and wake-side companion.
Each grey hair I pluck,
every inch that adds to my waistline,
and the stiffness of body that greets me
each morning reminds me of Death pending.
Unlike as a child,
when I did everything to hasten the aging process,
as an adult I do everything to retard vintage:
running every other day,
pushups and sit-ups in between.
But as the days shorten and get fewer,
exercising increasingly becomes work.
Death will not be denied.
In the safety of my home,
I switch on the television
and Death manifests itself.
A murder in a picket fence neighborhood,
 a drive-by shooting,
a plane crash,
famine in Somalia,
civil wars,
earthquakes,
hurricanes.
No place to hide,
unbashful Death is omnipresent.
To console myself,

I try to think I'm special.
Divinity has placed me on planet earth
for a certain cause that remains,
so my Death is not near.
But deep down I know I'm
swimming in my own delusion.
Death occupies me as much as sex.
But then again, maybe sex is both life and Death.
Sex must take place for either to occur.
My grandparents have long made peace with Death.
So are those of most of my friends.
Soon it will be my parents' turn,
and then it will be my turn,
or maybe in reverse.
When I see senior citizens,
another reminder of Death,
* I cannot help but try to imagine*
how they were in their youth.
I realize they too were children,
matured into adults, gave birth
to their own children, and now as grand-
or great-grandparents Death is imminent.
My heart goes out to them.
But it's a heavy heart sprinkled with sadness.
How could so much vigor, energy,
and unlimitedness convert to such lifelessness?
Notwithstanding, though, they are the lucky ones,
their less lucky contemporaries have long
joined the spirit world.
Considering the many ways to die,
* to have endured to the age of borrowed time*

is truly a remarkable accomplishment.
Respect is due.
I realize I'm soon to replace
the senior citizens of today.
There are so many deathtraps,
but we die only once.
Die, I must.
But Death, please, wait a while longer.
Though I've lived three lives,
I have so much more to experience.
Death, I know I've come a long way,
But Death, I've so much further to go.
I'm yet to pass on my genetic material
to the human pool,
the biggest contribution any of us
can make to mankind.
So Death, lend me more time,
occupy yourself elsewhere.
I know, Death, you are saying how foolish I am,
since both of us know that
life and Death are the same,
both are illusions within illusions.
I know you are saying why would anyone
want to live given the misery and tribulations of life,
compared with the peace of Death.
But Death, I'm only human.
I fear oblivion.
No one has come back from Death to tell me
how Death really is.
As a human I fear the unknown,
so I prefer to stick to life of which I know,

though I understand it not.
Death, I'm paying homage to you.
I'm living side by side with you.
I go to bed at night with you and I rise with you.
For doing that please reward me with a few more days.
Thank you.

SEVERAL YEARS AFTER I wrote this poem I read or viewed a television program (or was it my state of mind at the time that conjured up that theory, I'm not sure anymore) that said at a certain time in human evolution forty years represented the genetic life span of our ancestors. Meaning that few people lived beyond forty, and anyone older than forty would have been considered very old. It was sometime later an evolutionary breakthrough enabled or endowed human beings with the genetic capacity to live beyond forty years.

Coming upon this information or realization, I thought, so this is why at forty our genetic defects (heart diseases, colon cancer, diabetes, etc.) start showing up, and women start experiencing menopause, and that childbirth is such a problematic undertaking for women over thirty-five. It seems although this evolutionary breakthrough allowed us to live beyond our forties, at that age our bodies still go through a death process. At forty our bodies start to die. So it was no wonder that as I entered my thirties death occupied me as much as it did. My body and mind were preparing me for what in the distant past would have been my imminent death. We may not be dying at forty any longer, but apparently our bodies and minds still remember the days when we used to die at that age.

My first memory of death was at the age of seven when

my maternal grandfather died. I think back then I understood he would be gone. I remember most of the adults in my life (my mother, father and aunts) were busy with the death. I don't remember feeling sad or unhappy. I suspect I was neutral in my feelings about his death. I don't remember seeing his dead body, nor do I remember going to his funeral or being part of his wake. So I suspect that I was not yet fully aware of that thing called death.

Later, as I grew older, I would become more familiar with the alleged circumstances of my grandfather's death. My grandfather used to go to sea with a friend whom people said was a wicked obeah man. My grandfather noticed his friend never did shit on land. He always waited until the canoe was out at sea to shit. The friend didn't shit on land because he feared someone would pass behind him and use his feces to put obeah on him. One day my grandfather made some kind of joke with his friend about the fact that he never shits on land. This made his friend vex. Soon afterwards my grandfather fell sick, and he noticed a worm coming out of his head. He paid a visit to a *gadè*. The *gadè* told him that he had been poisoned and asked my grandfather whether anyone had given him anything shortly before he fell sick. My grandfather told him that the friend with whom he goes to sea had given him a bottle of honey. The *gadè* asked my grandfather to bring him the bottle of honey. When the *gadè* poured the honey on a tree bark, they noticed that it contained plenty particles of animal hair and skin; and in a few weeks the tree dried up and died. My grandfather never fully recovered from the poison, he was sick off and on until his death.

My grandfather's friend wasn't only evil, he was full of

mischief. He would send his children to run night errands and on their way home give them the scare of their life by appearing as a horse, a huge dog, or some other menacing creature.

My grandfather's friend, in turn, met his end at the hands of his wife. He had two look-alike bottles. One contained a poison, and the other a potion to protect himself against other people's obeah. To avoid any mixup, he kept the bottles at separate corners of the house. Tired of her husband's wickedness, one night when he was asleep, his wife switched bottles. In the morning her husband drank his dose of protection, but as the liquid trickled down his throat he cried out, "*Yo bien pwan mwen, yo bien pwan mwen!*" ("They well catch me, they well catch me!").

The second time death made his entry into my life was when our neighbor, the father of some of my playmates died. They said the man died from poison. The story was that although he owned and operated a passenger truck (meaning he wasn't the worst off), he was always accepting drinks from people, but never buying anyone drinks. So someone poured poison in his drink. This was the story I heard at the time. But then I was about eight, so there was probably more to the story than came my way.

With this death I became better acquainted with death. I viewed the body while it lay in the coffin, and I was there at the all-night wake during which mourners drank booze and coffee, danced *Kutumba*, and told stories. To this day I can still remember the rhythm the drummers played, and to this day my perception of an ideal wake is the one that took place at my neighbor's house. One with folk music, dancing, storytelling and booze. This death was close to me in distance, but not close to me emotionally. To me the dead man was simply the father of my playmates. I had felt no sadness. I had shed no tears.

I was nine years old and attending the Plain View Primary School, at La Ressource, Vieux Fort, when death made its third impression upon me. My ten-year-old school mate from Pierrot drowned while attempting to cross a raging river. This death was very disturbing, not only because we had lost a good cricketer and footballer but because at the time I wasn't associating death with people my age. To me, it was old people, people my parents' age and older who were supposed to die, not someone in my own age group. This death brought it home that, yes, death was a possibility even for those my age, and this was disturbing. The sense of unease that my schoolmate's death induced stayed with me for quite a while.

Since then there have been many other deaths, including the death of my maternal grandmother and the death of my father's siblings. However, when these deaths occurred I was away in America and I don't remember being particularly disturbed by them. Before my father's death, the last of my close family to die was my aunt who lived in Dennery — my mother's second oldest sister — who lost her will to live after her husband died. Her death had touched me, not so much out of an emotional attachment to her, but out of empathy with my cousins, her children, for the loss of both their parents in such a short time span.

Probably the only experience that came close to the death of my father in terms of this aching sense of irreversible loss was at eighteen months old when my mother departed for England, severing the mother-child bond. Indeed, given the pitiful, deplorable physical state I was in (according to what I was told), and the lasting, deleterious effect on my behavior and state of mind right through my childhood and adolescent years, for all practical purposes the separation must have felt like my mother had died, like I had lost a mother. However, I was too young when my mother left to remember the severity of the emotional pain I suffered, so I cannot realistically compare the pain of that experience with the pain of my father's death.

To find an experience I can objectively compare with the death of my father in terms of emotional distress, I have to turn not to a physical death, but to a broken heart, suffered when my live-in girlfriend of two years left me, the one whom I was sure would be my wife and the mother of my children. I was thirty-seven. When she left, I thought my heart would not hold up, I thought the morning would not find me in it. It was only then that I understood why so many people take their lives (in St. Lucia usually by hanging or drinking a herbicide) after their partners cheat on them, or ditch them. The pain is simply too much to bear. It's as though the separation or betrayal is worse than if the offending spouse had passed away. The betrayal itself becomes a kind of death, so taking one's own life is just a confirmation of what has already taken place.

Before my father's death, I thought I had made my peace with death. I thought I was mentally and emotionally prepared for my parents' death. And I thought that if I can live to tell the tale of the broken heart I suffered when my girlfriend broke up with me, then surely I can handle just about anything. For what could be worse than a broken heart? Okay, maybe I could not have handled the death of anyone of my brothers and sisters. Maybe I still hadn't reconciled myself to any of my siblings dying, but the possibility and hence fear of my parents dying had been a preoccupation since childhood. Now I know I was dealing in abstractions, I was informed by theory, not by reality. Now I know one can never be ready for death. Now I know I can never get used to the notion my father is no longer there. Now I know that, unlike girlfriends, fathers are irreplaceable.

People say you shall overcome. But how is that possible? How can I overcome the death of my father? No, it is not possible. Yes, I can carry on, I must carry on. But I cannot overcome his death. I cannot overcome the fact that my father is no longer there. To the contrary, what has enabled me to carry on is that I have never fully given in to the notion he is dead. On some level of my consciousness he is alive and well. To carry on, I have had to continue living a lie, so how can it be said I can overcome his death? No. That's not true.

So tell the insurance adjuster who placed a value of zero on my father's life that I cannot overcome my father's death. Tell the reckless god-playing driver who, as if agreeing with the insurance adjuster, reduced my father to a dirty ragged doll of no use to a child that I can never overcome my father's death. Tell them I wasn't ready for my father's death. Tell them I can never be ready for my father's death. Tell them I can never get used to the notion my father is no longer there. Tell them I want my father back.

My Father Was A Beekeeper

MY FATHER WAS A BEEKEEPER, so in preparing to write about him I consulted my mother on how he became interested in bees. She said that her own father had been a beekeeper and it was from accompanying her father on his visits to his hives that my dad became interested in bees. She wasn't clear how my father obtained his first hive; whether it was from her father or whether he got the bees from the wild. But she said that at first my father got into bees strictly as a hobby. He set up his first hive under a mango tree in the yard, and every afternoon after a day at the tailor shop he sat under the tree and studied the bees. He watched them as they flew out of the hive, and as they returned with their collection of nectar and pollen, trying to decipher where they went to do the collecting. He would open the hive to study how the bees made the wax and the honey, and to identify the queen, the workers and the drones. Clearly, my father's first engagement with bees wasn't out of financial need, but as a hobby, a study, an intellectual pursuit.

Of course, by the time my father had seven, eight children to feed, beekeeping was no longer just a pastime. It had become a serious undertaking that helped support his family. And in making a successful go at it, he became just as busy and industrious as the bees he was tending. Besides the harvesting and processing of the honey, and between the sewing, farming, trucking and preaching, my father was busy maintaining hives and tending bees: weekly visits to the hives, building the boxes called supers, that stacked up made up the hive, and making the frames (that hang in the supers) for holding the foundations or thin sheets of wax on which the bees build wax combs for storing their honey and pollen and for laying their eggs. Then there were post production activities, such as my mother retailing the honey by pint and quart bottles, and my father wholesaling it by multiple-gallon containers to buyers from as far as the neighboring island of Martinique.

But my father's attention to bees went beyond a means of supporting his family. He took great pleasure in explaining the ways of the bees to anyone who showed interest or who didn't have a choice but to listen. At church he built whole sermons around ants and bees, extolling their organization, industriousness and selflessness, not only as handiworks of God and models of Christian life but to say that if God can take care of such lowly creatures, how much more will He look after us if we put our trust in Him. For instance, he would reference Matthew, chapter 6, verses *26-29: "consider the fowls of the air: they sow not, neither do they reap, nor gather into barns,* yet God feeds them, much less we who are higher than them in God's pecking order. And how about the lilies of the field, they toil not, neither do they spin, but Solomon in all his glory and splendor could not touch them in beauty. So why despair when someone won't hire you because you refuse to work on the Sabbath of the Lord thy God? Don't you know that all you have to do is put your trust in God and he will do the rest?"

Growing up, for my father to get an opportunity to educate me about bees, he had to corner me because back then I took little interest in anything but sports, games and reading storybooks. And I didn't take too kindly to anything that came between me and these activities. So I didn't learn to sew like my older brothers, neither did I learn anything about the workings of motor vehicles, much less how to fix them. And whereas my older brothers were driving from the age of thirteen, I was nineteen but could barely drive, even though I already had a license, the acquisition of which my father had arranged without me having to take the exam. An act he probably regretted, as I was a big embarrassment and disappointment to him when, on our way home from the police station, straight after receiving my driver's license, I grazed his vehicle against a truck parked street-side a few yards from the police station.

Unfortunately for me, the place my father usually cornered me to pass on this family tradition of beekeeping was uphill, under the bush, overlooking the Caribbean Sea and the American-built dock, next to an open beehive, me smoking the bees, he unhurriedly examining the hive or extracting the honey-filled frames. There, speaking to me through his veil with great appetite and in confidential tones, as if I'm the only one with whom he was allowed to share the secret of the bees, or as if he would incur the wrath of the bees if they caught wind of him revealing their secrets, my father explained the ways of the bees, each time as if for the first time.

"You see. You must place the hive up from the ground. You can put it on stones, or you can build a platform for it. You don't want the bottom of the hive to rot and you don't want a downpour to wash away the hive. Not only that. The bees have enemies. Bees are one of frogs' favorite foods. Frogs can destroy a hive in no time. Then there are mice. They dig holes to enter the hive where they make their nest. That's why it's a good idea to put the hive up from the ground."

At the mention of toads (frogs) I hurriedly looked around, as I was very afraid of these ugly creatures, more afraid of them than I was of bees. Ever since I have known myself I have always had nightmares in which a huge ugly toad jumps on me. Each time I would scream, waking up the house and bringing my dad to my bedside. But I can't remember us ever finding a toad in my bed. Once, though, we found a cat in my bedroom and, convinced it was a *jan gajé*, a disguised witch, taking no chances, my mother knocked it unconscious, placed it in a bucket, doused it with kerosene, and set it on fire.

Before opening the hive, my father attempts to calm the bees by smoking the entrance of the hive and then all around it. Then using a flat metal implement, a pinch bar of sorts, he uncaps the cover of the hive and lifting it slightly, smokes inside the hive with the hope that by the time he completely removes the cover, the bees will be subdued. Once the cover is completely off, he gives the hive a full smoke treatment.

Through all of this, and above the energetic buzzing of the bees, he continues his conversation.

"There are three kinds of bees in the hive. The workers, the drones, and the queen. Most of what you are seeing there are workers. They are the smallest bees in the hive. They are the girls or women of the hive, but they cannot make babies. You see how their behinds are pointed? That's their stinger. All worker bees sting, that's their weapon to guard against intruders that come to eat the bees or drink their honey. So when they bite you, don't be too angry, they are just doing their job. You notice that when a bee bites you a piece of it stays with the sting? Well, that means every bee that bites you dies in the process."

"Well, good," I thought, "that means I'm the first and last person they will bite."

"The drones, on the other hand, don't sting. Their only job is to mate with the queen, make baby bees with her. So as soon as they mate with the queen, they drop dead. And when there isn't enough food to go around, such as during the rainy season and during winter in cold countries when the bees can't go out to collect nectar and pollen, the workers kick the drones out of the hive where they soon die."

With the cover completely off, and having filled the hive completely with smoke, my father hands me the smoker to continue smoking the bees while he gets down to work. Smoke or no smoke the bees are in uproar at this assault, this invasion, and their angry, dizzying buzz strikes fear in my heart, informing me in no uncertain terms that today they will take no prisoners. They sting my hands, the hands holding onto the smoker, at will and quite a few climb under my veil and give various parts of my head the same treatment.

Noticing my not-too-calm reaction to the bees' stings, my father advises me to stay still, because the more I moved around the more the bees will bite me. I wished my father would stop talking and hurry up, but seemingly unmindful of the bee stings, he continues at a leisurely pace, just as when he was walking through his farm, personally greeting every plant and animal by name.

"When I tell you the drones are lazy, they are really lazy. They don't do a single thing around the nest. The baby worker bees must climb out of their brood cells all by themselves, but not the drones. It is the workers that must help the baby drones out of theirs. The drones don't even feed themselves. It is the workers that must spoon-feed them for them to stay alive.

"It doesn't pay to be lazy. You see how much honey we're taking out today? That's because no other creature works harder than the worker bee. They guard the nest against all intruders, they fly as far as two to three miles to collect pollen and nectar from flowers, they process the nectar into honey, they produce wax with which they make the honeycomb, they keep the hive clean by carrying all rubbish, dead bees and other dead insects out of the hive, and they also nurse and feed the broods or baby bees. Besides nectar and pollen, the workers also collect a glue-like substance from plants, called propolis, that they use to cement holes and cracks in the hive. The workers also use propolis to seal off dead animals too big for them to carry out. A few years ago I found a mouse inside the hive encased in propolis. Did you know that bees collect water too? Yes. They collect water. They use the water to dilute food for the broods, and during hot days they fan the water to cool down the hive."

"*No other creatures work harder than the worker bees!?*" a voice screams inside me as the bees continued their unmerciful attack. "Come on, how about us your children, carrying bananas, fertilizer, ground provisions, mangoes, golden apple, breadnut; making copra, collecting wood for the oven, making bricks and shoveling sand for the church building; carrying dung and dirt to cover rocks in the yard; and look, we are here carrying honey, extracting honey, squeezing honey, bees biting us every which way. All that, and we're not working harder than the bees! Whose side are you on?"

"Some people think that the bees are making honey for them, but that's far from the truth. When the bees gather pollen and nectar, they eat some right away but store the rest in the comb in the form of honey so that during bad weather, such as in the rainy season, when they cannot go out and collect food or when there aren't much flowers around, they can still have food to eat. That is why when you are extracting honey, you must always leave enough in the hive for the bees to live on."

As my father is talking, he pulls up a honey frame from the hive and, using twigs from a nearby tree, he brushes away the bees clinging to the frame, then examines it to ascertain the amount of honey it contains and to ensure the bees have sealed the honey; if it is not yet sealed, then it means the honey isn't ready for harvesting. When he is satisfied with one frame, he puts it in an empty box on the ground beside him, and pulls up another frame from the hive. The more honey he steals from the hive, the angrier and more active the bees become and the harder and faster I pump the smoker.

"Look at these bees over there, those with the large heads and bulging eyes. You see them? They are slightly bigger than the workers. These are the drones. As I told you before, they are the fathers of the hive but they don't do any work. Their only job is to make children with the queen. You see, when the queen is ready to make children, she goes on a flight far from the hive and the drones must follow the queen to mate with her in the air. The drones' big eyes are to make sure they don't lose track of the queen while on her mating flight. Now, since a hive has only one queen at a time, it is difficult to locate a queen, and they are usually in the bottom super, the brood chamber. I could take off the top supers to try to show you the queen, but I don't want to disturb the bees too much. But the way you can tell a queen from the other bees is that she is larger than them and has a slender, torpedo-like shape, kind of like a wasp. She has a stinger, so her behind is pointed like that of the workers, but she only uses it to sting and kill other queens."

My mind wanders in and out of my father's bee conversation. And that was to be expected, not only because of my lack of interest and the intermittent bee stings, but also because I have always been absentminded. So absentminded that as a child I was always losing or misplacing things such as pencils, exercise books, and my shoes, especially when I took them off to play soccer. In that regard I was a real mess of a child and was a source of great consternation to my mother. Up to today, I lose anything that isn't glued to my body, so I have no luck with pens, watches, hats, flash drives and umbrellas. Because of such absentmindedness I was accident-prone, and had developed a reputation for having bad luck. Anytime I attempted something risky, such as climbing a coconut tree, my siblings would echo, "Anderson, you know you have bad luck and you there climbing that tree!" Besides being a dreamer, my mind was always more in the past than in the present. In fact, my absentmindedness and preoccupation with the past, with what was wrong with me, were some of the reasons school didn't work as well for me as it should and why I took a dislike to it.

Amid my father's bee conversation, I would wonder whether we would finish harvesting the honey before nightfall in time to play a game of football or cricket, or to play marbles or tops or *kabowé* (wooden toy trucks), depending on what sport or game was in season at the time. Other times my mind would be on the novel I was reading and how it would end, or on the problems I was having at home or at school, such as being afraid of my mother, not wanting her for my mother, that nobody cared about me, nobody loved me. Or my mind would be on the Indian girl at school from Augier whom I liked, and the love note I had written to her to which I hadn't received a reply. Obviously, I had much bigger fish to fry than the ways of the bees.

"I came from England with several books on bees. I wish I still had them for you to read. But I lent them out and never got them back. Some of what I'm telling you there are from those books."

"Have I told you about swarming? Well, you see, when the bees have multiplied and become too many for the hive, the queen along with half of the bees will leave the hive and go look for another home to start a new colony. This is what they call swarming. The queen and the group of bees who leave the hive are called a swarm. Sometimes when you find a pack of bees resting on a tree branch or on an electric wire or post, this is what has happened. Don't mind the bees; they are very smart. The hive cannot stay without a queen. All the bees in the hive will leave if there is no queen. So just before the bees swarm, the workers will build about a dozen queen cells, which are bigger than the cells used to make the drones and the workers. The queen will then lay eggs in these cells. Mind you, these eggs are no different than the eggs used for the worker bees. But by feeding the larvae a special protein diet of what is called royal jelly they grow into queens, and all through life this is all the queens eat."

Enveloped by a profusion of cactus, palm trees, *bwa kanpèch, bwa d'owanj, tibonm,* white cedar, gum and other deciduous trees, we were in what can be described as a monastic bee sanctuary, so my father's lecture on the way of the bees was right at home. In fact, with my daydreaming and my wanting to be anywhere else but there, I was the only one out of place, out of order. Besides toads and mice, the bees had plenty of company. The bush was home to many species of birds, including hummingbirds, blackbirds, *toutwels* (wood doves) and *zatolans* (ground doves). Above the buzzing of the bees, bird calls filled the sanctuary and hummingbirds suckling nectar from cactus fruits were all about us. The sound of mongoose scuttling through the undergrowth announced that they too took residence in this monastic bee sanctuary.

"As soon as the eggs are laid," continued my father, "and before they hatch, the bees swarm. But now the bees have a problem. There can only be one queen in the hive. So the first queen that comes out of its cell will try to kill as many of the baby queens before they come out of theirs. She will do so by stinging them through the walls of their brood cells. All those that manage to hatch, including the firstborn, will fight among themselves to the death, leaving the victor as the only reigning queen of the hive. If there is a draw between the last two standing queens, there will be another swarm with one of the queens leaving with half of the remaining bees.

"About a week after the victorious queen emerges from her cell, it will be time for her to mate. To do so she flies some distance away from the hive where she is joined by a gathering of drones ready to mate with her. I think I have mentioned to you before that, for the drones, mating the queen is an act of suicide, because every drone that is able to mate with the queen dies, as part of its body gets ripped off in the process. After two or three of these mating flights, the queen will have enough fertilized eggs to lay for the rest of her life. She lives longer than any of the other bees. She can live up to five years, whereas the workers live only about a month, and the drones maybe a bit longer. Through most of the queen's life, she will lay about 1,500 eggs a day.

"Have I told you that when things are hard, for example, when there is a shortage of food in the hive, the worker bees drive out the drones who, without a hive, soon die? You know what this means? It doesn't pay to be lazy. A lazy man is a hungry man. And as your mother always tells you all, she has never seen work kill anybody."

And here I am, thinking how nice it would be to be a drone. To have all the time in the world to read, fly kites, play football, cricket, marbles, *toupee* (spinning top), and *kabowé* to my heart's content, while other people wash my clothes, clean my room, and even spoon-feed me. Life is so unfair.

"I hope you're listening carefully to what I'm saying. Because if I get sick or something was to happen to me, it is you and your brothers who will have to take over from me.

"Do you know that bees talk to each other? Yes. I tell you bees are very smart creatures. God knew what He was doing when he made them. When the bees come back from the field with their collection of honey and pollen, they land right there at the front of the hive and do a dance with their wings to tell the other bees in the hive how far away they found the food, how much of it is there and how to get to it. This way more bees can fly out and collect from this new source of food."

My final ordeal comes when my father has finished filling the box on the ground with honey frames. He helps me lift the honey-filled box onto my head on top of a cloth pad, and without delay I hasten to carry the honey through the bush along a narrow path to the little hut close to the road, where we remove the honey from the honey comb using a honey extractor, a cylindrical machine that works with centrifugal force. I have to hurry because not only is the box heavy and uncomfortable on my head, but I'm at the mercy of the bees. No matter how many sting me, I can do nothing to ease my discomfort, getting the honey safely to the extraction point is my number one priority.

I arrive at the hut relieved I made it with the honey box intact and glad to get a respite from my father's bee talk and from the firing line of bees. One of my brothers quickly unloads me. I will get a long breather. Another one of my brothers will return with an empty box to my father and will take my place beside him as he removes honey-filled frames from other hives. Like the beehives, there is division of labor in our camp. One of us stays with our dad under the bush and brings back the honey. Meanwhile, one or two others unseal the honey in the frame by slicing through the surface of the honey with a long knife (unsealing knife) specifically designed for that purpose. Then another places a frame in each of the two chambers of the honey extractor and by way of a handle, spins the machine to extract the honey, which collects at the bottom of the machine. The accumulated honey is then strained into containers. The extractor was a welcome relief, because before my father acquired it, we had to cut out the honeycomb from the frames and spend hours manually squeezing the honey out of the combs, with bees, long thought dead, stinging our hands at will.

WHEN MY FATHER WAS ALIVE I didn't take much interest in bees and I saw his bee operation as keeping me away from my own preoccupations; but in writing about him, I knew I had to write about bees because they were such a big part of his life and I felt compelled to research, to uncover what about bees so fascinated my father, that sat so well with things inside him that he spent a lifetime studying, caring for them. Was it because the bees gave him a good excuse to get away from everything (the injustices of the world, the hardships and struggles of life, the challenges of raising a family) and be at peace with himself, be alone with his thoughts, become one with nature? Was it that being alone with the bees allowed him to meditate and contemplate the goodness of God, to commune with God, even? Was it because, contemplating the ways of the bees, he drew lessons to guide his life and enrich his relationship with his God?

Or was it that beekeeping—maintaining hives, providing an environment that allowed the bees to flourish, to be even more productive than they would be unattended in the wild—sat so well with his loving and caring nature? Was it that the industriousness of the bees, the giving of self, was so much in tune with what his life was about? The worker bees toiling ceaselessly for the good of the colony, guarding the hive against intruders and invaders with their sting and the certainty of their death; the drones zealously performing their sole function of mating the queen, ensuring the longevity and perpetuity of the hive, unmindful that this very act spells their doom?

My father always lectured us on helping each other, sticking by each other, protecting each other. Was it from studying the life of bees that he developed such family values, and did his fascination with bees have something to do with a bee colony's organization, cooperation, coordination and order? Every single bee with a prescribed function: the drones to mate the queen, the queen to populate the hive. Young workers (one to twelve days old) acting as nurses, tending and feeding the brood of unborn bees, fashioning pollen into a kind of bread for supplying nourishment to the brood; acting as scavengers and undertakers, keeping the hive clean and free of dead bees and other insects; and acting as soldiers, guarding the hive with their very lives. Middle-aged workers (twelve to twenty days old), the factories of the hive, constructing the comb, processing nectar into honey, and storing the honey and pollen in special honey and pollen cells; and acting as air conditioning units, ventilating the hive with the flapping of their wings. Mature bees (twenty days and older), the colony's foragers or food gatherers, collecting all the nectar, pollen, propolis, and water that the hive uses, and providing the enzymes needed for converting the nectar into honey.

Or was it that the bees mirrored my father's disposition towards his family, his Seventh Day Adventist flock, his community at large, or life in general? The notion that a life should be lived not just for self, that a life should be of value, of usefulness not just to one's immediate family, but also to one's community, to one's country, to the world at large? The notion "you are your brother's keeper," your neighbor is anyone in need, and you should do unto others as you would like them do unto you? In the course of my research, I discovered that, indeed, the bees' industriousness serves not just the colony, or bees and honey thieves like bears, wasps, moths and toads, but is of great service to man. So although I cannot be sure what about bees so fascinated my father, I know he would have been hard-pressed to find another creature that had so many lessons to teach, and contributed so much to the world at large.

Consider, for example, honey, pollen, and royal jelly. Pollen and royal jelly contain protein, and all three contain carbohydrates, fatty acids, enzymes, vitamins, minerals, and water—all the substances needed to sustain life. Moreover, they are the only foods found to contain pinocembrin, an antioxidant associated with improved brain function.

Nutrition aside, these substances along with propolis, another product of the bees, are thought of as wonder drugs that boost the immune system and improve blood flow; provide treatment for common cold, sore throat, diabetic ulcer, asthma, diarrhea, lethargy, nausea, insomnia, low libido, anemia, cancer, high cholesterol, constipation, burns, superficial wounds and all types of infection; prevent colon damage, cancer and heart diseases; and remove parasites such as worms from the body.

Beeswax, another product of bees, is used to make crayons and candles. It is said the Catholic Church alone uses one million pounds of beeswax per year for making candles. In woodwork and industry, beeswax is used as a polisher, a sealant, a lubricant and as a waterproofing and waxing agent. In food processing, it is used as coating for cheese, candies and pills. In cosmetics, it is used as a hair hardener (for example, in dreadlocks), and in lipstick, lip balm, soaps, hand and body cream, and in organic balms and ointments. Beeswax is also used as an industrial absorbent. Combined with certain enzymes it is used to clean oil spills, where the wax absorbs the oil and the enzymes break it down to render it harmless.

Yet notwithstanding the inherent value of bee products, it is in their role as pollinators that bees are of greatest value to man. For example, the American Institute of Biological Sciences reported that insect pollination produces some US$40 billion worth of products annually in the United States alone. So vital are honeybees to US agricultural production, that commercial beekeepers are contracted to migrate their hives, following the bloom from south to north, to provide pollination for many different crops. So much so that for many US beekeepers their main source of income isn't from honey production but from the pollination services their hives provide.

One study (Science Daily: Sep. 15, 2008) estimated the worldwide annual economic value of insect pollination at US$217 billion. A second study (by INRA and CNRS French scientists and a UFZ German scientist) placed this figure at €153 billion in 2005. All told, insect pollinators contribute to one-third of the world's diet, and the honeybee accounts for 80 percent of all pollination done by insects. Therefore, as some have put it, one of every three mouthfuls of food we eat depends directly or indirectly on pollination by honey-bees. So whether we have never tasted a bee product nor used any formulation that contains bee products, we cannot help but benefit from the life of bees.

Apparently, my father understood the value and impor-tance of bees. In fact, he respected the value and sanctity of all life. He not only understood and appreciated the value of bees, he revered bees, he gloried in their industriousness, incredulousness, and miraculousness. His life mirrored the life of bees. Even in old age his life was of tremendous value to his family, to his Adventist flock, to his friends and ac-quaintances and to his community at large. Up till today, I meet people (some my age, some older, some slightly younger) who would inform me with great emotion in their voices how it was a piece of advice from my father that had changed their lives for the better, or had led them to the fi-nancial success they were now enjoying, or had saved their lives, even.

So this is why I couldn't fathom how an insurance ad-juster could place a value of zero on my father's life. Or how, as if in concurrence, some reckless, god-playing twenty-four-year-old motorist could reduce my father to a throw-away doll, of use not even to a lonely child. I wonder now if the insurance adjuster and the god-playing driver had knowl-edge of the life of bees, and had a sense that, in terms of use-fulness and selflessness, my father's life matched that of bees, what value would they have placed on his life. Maybe with such knowledge my father's life would have been spared, and I would not have had to listen to the insurance adjuster's foolishness about life expectancy and income stream as measures of value; nor would I have been exposed to the god-playing driver's handshake that seemed to say "a deed well done."

My Father Was The Last Of His Line

MY FATHER WAS THE LAST OF HIS LINE. For by the time he met his death, or rather by the time death met him, his grandparents were dead, his mother and father were dead, his uncles and aunts were dead, his brothers and sisters were all dead.

What does this mean: he was the last of his line? I'm not sure what it all means, but to me it makes his death an even greater tragedy. The image that comes to mind is the passing away of the last member of a tribe, the last native speaker of a language, the last member of a generation, the last plant or animal of a species. Extinction. A permanent, unrecoverable loss to the world. Something, someone, a language, a culture, a people, never again to be seen, heard or experienced.

Now, I know that my father was survived by all his nine children and all his grandchildren and most of his nieces and nephews, so technically speaking he wasn't the last of his line. But since he was the last of his siblings to pass away, and since by the time of his death his parents and aunts and uncles were long dead, to me it feels that he was the last of his line. It is the only way I can express it to convey the gravity of his death to me, to capture the emotional impact his death had on me. So "my father was the last of his line" may not be the actual truth but it is the emotional truth.

Not long after my father's death, I met a man who told me he was my cousin. I had never seen this man before, much less knew he was my cousin. But, yes, he was my cousin and he knew my father well. He said: "You wouldn't know that by our last names, even if you were to research the lineage, because people long ago were very careless about their last names. They had a curious habit of adopting their father's first name, or sometimes even their grandfather's first name as their last name. This eccentricity made it difficult to trace lineages."

My cousin said that he knew more about his lineage than most relatives his age because he had been raised by his grandmother. His mother was from Grace, Vieux Fort, but before he was born she moved to a job in Castries. When he was a year old, he fell and injured his head, so his mother took him to Grace to his grandmother's home for healing. After he recovered his mother wanted to return to Castries with him, but his grandmother said, "No way, I'm not allowing this child out of my sight, he must stay here with me." So this was how he came to be raised by his grandmother instead of his mother.

His grandmother loved to talk about the past. She told him my father's great-great-grandfather was a slave named

Jn. Baptiste. It wasn't quite clear whether Jn. Baptiste had arrived in St. Lucia straight from Africa or from a neighboring island or even whether he was born a slave. But in 1838, emancipation found Jn. Baptiste a slave.

According to legend Jn. Baptiste was a strong and proud man, and although he was a slave the plantation owner had great respect for him. For, you see, Jn. Baptiste had protection. He had a *ti bolom*, which, as described earlier, is a toddler-size supernatural being that does its master's bidding, including protecting him. I don't know where or when Jn. Baptiste acquired this ti bolom, whether it accompanied him from Africa or whether he found it this side of the Atlantic. As it happened, Jn. Baptiste's wife was a rude and headstrong woman. An unhealthy attitude for a slave, especially one who was a house slave. Whenever Jn. Baptiste's wife was rude to the master's wife and the master threatened to punish her, the ti bolom would bring Jn. Baptiste the news and Jn. Baptiste would in turn have a word with the master. As a result, despite the rudeness of Jn. Baptiste's wife, she was never whipped nor punished in any way. Clearly, because of Jn. Baptiste's supernatural powers the master was afraid of his ability to do him harm.

Jn. Baptiste had several children, one of whom was a son named Antoine Jn. Baptiste, who begot a son named Reynolds Antoine, who, besides two illegitimate children, begot Hubert Reynolds, Myese Antoine, Felix Reynolds, Marie Reynolds and Raymond Reynolds. Hubert Reynolds in turn begot Alexander Reynolds, Matilda Reynolds, Eldica Reynolds, St. Brice Reynolds (my father) and Andrew Jean Reynolds (the lawyer and politician). St. Brice Reynolds (my father) begot nine children, six boys and three girls. St. Brice

Reynolds outlived all his brothers and sisters, including his eldest sister, who was of a different father.

That eldest sister died in 1960, two years after my birth, so I never got to know her. Of my dad's other siblings, who shared the same father (and mother) with him, Eldica died in the 1970s, Matilda died in 1985, Jean Reynolds died in 1987, and Alexander died in 1992. So since 1992 my father had been the last remaining member of his immediate family, the last of his line. A line that could be traced back to Jn. Baptiste, the powerful slave with his very own personal supernatural security guard, whose own slave master held him in awe.

My father was the last of his line, yet the insurance adjuster said he had no value. My father was the last of his line, yet he was extinguished in the name of recklessness. That the god-playing motorist who took his life was driving with abundant recklessness, there is no doubt. Here is the sworn testimony of the one and only eye witness to the accident that took my father's life. The eye witness who also happened to be the same person who had tried to flag me down as I bypassed the scene of my father's death on my way to work in Castries, but, apparently, wanting no part of it, I drove all the way to Castries, only to turn around, in the middle of my coffee brew, to meet death.

ON THURSDAY 6 JUNE, 2002, *about 6:30 a.m., I left my home for work driving my motor car with Registration Number* (omitted). *I left my yard and turned left onto the St. Jude's Highway, traveling in the direction of Vieux Fort town. It was raining when I left home.*

As I approached the Cantonement bus shelter, I saw a man

cross from the bus shelter on the right side to the left side of the road and continue walking on the left side of the road. As I was in the process of passing the man, I saw a blue car, traveling in the opposite direction towards St. Jude Hospital at a fast speed, leave its side and come to my side of the road. I slowed down and moved to my left side. The oncoming car then passed in front of my car, hitting the left front, and continued past my car on my left off the road, by which time I had brought my car to a halt.

I came out of my car and saw that the blue car had come to a stop on the left side of the road towards St. Jude Hospital. I then went to an area in front of a concrete wall where I saw the same man who I earlier mentioned on the ground off the road in front of the wall. He lives a few yards away from me and his name is St. Brice Reynolds, aka "Seedwan." The ambulance came shortly afterwards and conveyed Mr. Reynolds to the hospital.

The police arrived sometime afterwards and took measurements in the presence of the driver of the blue car (name of driver omitted) *and myself. Whilst on the scene the police officer informed us that Mr. Reynolds had died.*

As a result of the impact with the blue motor car with Registration Number (omitted), *my car sustained the following damages: broken left head lamp and left indicator, dented fender and bumper.*

ACCORDING TO THIS REPORT, traveling north, the god-playing motorist was going so fast and was so out of control that he completely left his side of the road, hit the extreme left of an oncoming vehicle (traveling south), yet was still able to pick up my dad who was strolling along the side of the road and crush him against a perimeter wall twenty or twenty-five feet away from the road.

How do you explain this? How do you reconcile this?

How do you come to grips with this grim reality? Some people say his time had come. Some say God is Master, it was all part of His master plan, no matter how bad it may feel or look, it happened for the best. Some say he didn't suffer and he went out before senility and sickness could strip him of his independence and dignity. He had a good life, some say. He was an outstanding member of his community. For sure there is a place waiting for him in the kingdom of God. One couldn't wish for any better way to go. Rather than mourn his death, we should celebrate his life.

As for me, my faith in God isn't that strong. I believe in behavior, conduct, habits and probability. If one habitually drives recklessly, with or without the help of God or Devil, chances are it won't be long before one kills oneself and/or other people. This is what I believe. It is one thing to give up your life for a cause or to save someone's life, but it is a whole different story to forfeit your life because someone is trying to get to his destination a few minutes sooner. The wastefulness of my father's death, I cannot reconcile, I cannot come to grips with. No. I cannot.

So tell the motorist who killed my father, reducing him to a worthless dirty doll, for the thrill of a fast drive or for a shot of rum or for getting to work or to his girlfriend a few minutes sooner, my father was the last of his line.

Tell the insurance adjuster who insinuated my father was dead long before the god-playing motorist committed violence on him, and as such was without value, not even salvage value, my father was the last of his line.

MY BROTHER, the economics professor, the one who gave the eulogy at my father's funeral, lives in Ohio, on the outskirts of Cincinnati, a city named after an Indian tribe that no longer exists. With the same ruthlessness that the twenty-four-year-old rubbed-off my father, the Europeans decimated the Indian nations because they were in the way of so-called progress and civilization. To them, the Indians and their way of life were of zero or negative value. In turn the Europeans, once again playing god, named their cities, rivers, and sports clubs after the Indians. What, if anything, will the insurance adjuster and the god-playing motorist name after my father, I wonder?

A day after my brother returned to Ohio from my father's funeral, his wife gave birth to their second child, a son whom they named Bricen, in memory of his grandfather, my father, St. Brice Reynolds, just as my dad had named my last brother, my last sibling, after our grandfather. Bricen is one grandchild who will never see, never hear, never know his grandfather, and my father is one grandfather who will never see, never hear, never know this grandson.

So again, I would like to tell the god-playing motorist and the insurance adjuster, both of whom had taken it upon themselves to determine who lives, who dies and who is worth what, that my father was the last of his line. I would like to ask them, what value would they place on a grandchild knowing his grandfather or a grandfather feasting his eyes on his grandchild?

I would like to tell them of this old man who once told me it was only when he started having grandchildren that he felt his journey on earth complete, he began to acquire a feeling of well-being, he felt assured his seed, his lineage will perpetuate, and he began to glimpse immortality. What value would the motorist and the insurance adjuster place on that? I wonder.

Who Was My Father

Who was my father?
My father was a tailor.
My father was a beekeeper.
My father was a banana farmer.
My father was a trucker.

Who was my father?
My father was a Seventh Day Adventist.
My father was a preacher.
My father was the elder of his church.
My father was a man of God.
My father walked with God.

Who was my father?
My father was a brave man.
My father was a hero.
My father was a loving man.

My father was a compassionate man.
My father was a forgiving man.
My father was a man with a kind heart.
My father was a long-suffering man.

Who was my father?
My father was an intelligent man.
My father was an intellectual.
My father was a patient man.
My father was a quiet man.
My father was a peaceful man.
My father was a man who placed a high value on his peace
of mind.

Who was my father?
My father was a man with two brothers and three sisters.
My father was a married man.
My father was a family man.
My father was a husband.
My father was a man with nine children.
My father was a man with six boys and three girls.
My father was the last of his line.

But who was my father?

The World of Anderson Reynolds

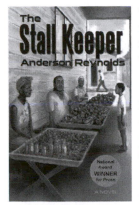

The Stall Keeper is an engaging narrative that readers of all ages will find both informative and climactic... An excellent aid to our understanding of our past."
— The Voice

In Dr. Reynolds St. Lucia has produced another writer of the calibre, or of even deeper essence than Nobel Laureate V. S. Naipaul **— Peter Lansiquot, CARICOM economist and diplomat**

"The Stall Keeper is arguably the best novel to come out of St. Lucia." **— Mc Donald Dixon, novelist, poet, and playwright**

" ... a wonderful journey down memory lane for anyone who has breathed the salty sea breeze of Vieux Fort in the middle and late 20th century... It's a wry book; a story that sticks in the mind."
— Jolien Harmsen, author of A History of St. Lucia

"*The Struggle for Survival* is an important road map of St. Lucia in the pre and post independence period."
— Sir John Compton, Prime Minister of St. Lucia

"a 206 paged gem ... a powerful commentary ... A deep sincere analytical look into the state of things in the island today. *The Struggle For Survival* is truly a compendium of St. Lucian life from early times to the modern era ... "
—Modeste Downes, author of *Phases*

"... an invaluable book...a source of much information. Much scholarly research has gone into the writing of this work. In a very definite way, establishes the Saint Lucian personality, the Saint Lucian national and cultural identity."
—Jacques Compton, Author of *a troubled dream*

The Struggle For Survival, although obviously well researched, is an easy-to-read intriguing story of the social and political development of St. Lucia. **—Travis Weekes, Author of *Let There Be Jazz***

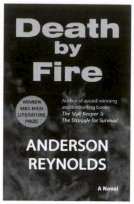

"Death by Fire is an impressive piece of narration ... A veritable tapestry of St. Lucian life and culture ... Easily one of the most compelling pieces of literature I have laid hands on in recent years."
— **Modeste Downes, author of *Phases***

"The telling of the story is exceptional ... A cunningly-woven tale ... A journey back into St. Lucian life ... (which) paints the dark side of the struggle for survival in a young country." — **The Voice**

"A novel on a grand scale ... A broad canvas of St. Lucian life ... If one is looking for a key to the feeling and conscience of the age in which we live, this novel is a guide."
—**The Crusader**

www.jakoproductions.com

Anderson Reynolds was born and raised in Vieux Fort, St. Lucia, where he now resides. He holds a PhD in Food and Resource Economics from the University of Florida. He is the author of three other award-winning and national best-selling books, namely the novels *The Stall Keeper* and *Death by Fire* and the creative non-fiction *The Struggle For Survival: an historical, political, and socioeconomic perspective of St. Lucia*. Dr. Reynolds' books and newspaper and magazine articles have established him as one of St. Lucia's most prominent and prolific writers and a foremost authority on its socioeconomic history.